CURB TRADING ON BROAD STREET, NEW YORK

The Stock Exchange is shown on the left. In the background, a statue
of Washington stands in front of the Sub-Treasury

ISBN 978-1-330-08016-0
PIBN 10020722

1 MONTH OF
FREE
READING

at

www.ForgottenBooks.com

By purchasing this book you are eligible for one month membership to ForgottenBooks.com, giving you unlimited access to our entire collection of over 700,000 titles via our web site and mobile apps.

To claim your free month visit:

www.forgottenbooks.com/free20722

WHAT EVERY BUSINESS WOMAN
SHOULD KNOW

WHAT
EVERY BUSINESS WOMAN
SHOULD KNOW

A COMPLETE GUIDE
TO BUSINESS USAGES AND REQUIREMENTS
WITH EXPLANATIONS OF BUSINESS TERMS
AND COMMERCIAL FORMS

BY

L. C. KEARNEY

ILLUSTRATED WITH DIAGRAMS AND PHOTOGRAPHS

NEW YORK
FREDERICK A. STOKES COMPANY
PUBLISHERS

CURB TRADING ON BROAD STREET, NEW YORK

The Stock Exchange is shown on the left. In the background, a statue
of Washington stands in front of the Sub-Treasury

WHAT
EVERY BUSINESS WOMAN
SHOULD KNOW

A COMPLETE GUIDE
TO BUSINESS USAGES AND REQUIREMENTS
WITH EXPLANATIONS OF BUSINESS TERMS
AND COMMERCIAL FORMS

BY

L. C. KEARNEY

ILLUSTRATED WITH DIAGRAMS AND PHOTOGRAPHS

NEW YORK
FREDERICK A. STOKES COMPANY
PUBLISHERS

40220

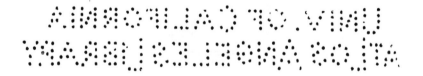

PUBLISHERS' NOTE

This book is the same in every respect as WHAT EVERY BUSINESS MAN SHOULD KNOW, with the exception of a few subjects which pertain exclusively to women.

If a man can write a better book, preach a better sermon, or make a better mousetrap than his neighbor, though he build his house in the woods, the world will make a beaten path to his door.

PREFACE

There are assembled in this book, arranged for convenient reference in encyclopedic form, commercial terms and data which the American Business Woman who desires to establish herself as a factor in what has heretofore been considered "the affairs of men" should know.

It has been the endeavor to present as authentic information upon each subject as could be obtained. The World Almanac, McClure's Magazine, the Postal Telegraph & Cable Company, Western Union Telegraph Company, Adams Express Company, Yawman & Erbe Mfg. Company, Harper & Brothers, and the New York Telephone Company have either graciously contributed or approved the subject matter accredited to them. Funk & Wagnalls' *New Standard Dictionary* has been a helpful guide in forming certain definitions.

In all lines, the Business Woman will find it desirable to be conversant with financial terms, and the most important of these have been fully covered. A recognized authority in the financial world, Montgomery Rollins, Esq., of the "House of Rollins" (New York, Boston, Philadelphia, Chicago, San Francisco, Los Angeles and London) kindly permitted use of the quotations taken from his works on Finance.

Particular attention is directed to the article on "Difference in Time." No other publication, it is believed, contains so complete and up-to-date a table of Standard Railroad Time which the various foreign countries have adopted in recent years as appears under this caption. To Mr. W. F. Allen, of the American Railway Association, who in 1883 successfully solved the problem of a standardized time for the railroads in the United States, is due grateful acknowledgment for having supplied the data to bring this subject to date.

How shall I properly write this check? What is the shortest and cheapest way I can telegraph my message? How many ways can I invest my savings? How shall I start a filing system? What does that abbreviation stand for? What are "Bulls and Bears"? Shall I send by parcel post or express? What is a Letter of Credit? A Traveler's check? How shall I become a Notary Public? What is a Power of Attorney? These are a few questions the answers to which will be found in this book. That Business Women will find it a convenient and complete reference book is the author's hope.

L. C. KEARNEY.

CONTENTS

CONTENTS

CONTENTS

WHAT EVERY BUSINESS WOMAN
SHOULD KNOW

Abbreviations

A.	Acres
A. B. or B. A.	Bachelor of Arts
Abp. or Archp.	Archbishop
A. C.	(Ante Christum) Before Christ
Acct. or a/c	Account
A. D.	(Anno Domini) Year of our Lord
Adj.	Adjective
Adjt.	Adjutant
Adjt.-Gen.	Adjutant-General
Ad. lib.	(Ad libitum) At pleasure
Adm.	Administrator; Admiral
Admx.	Administratrix
Adv.	Adverb; Advent: Advertisement
A. G. F. A.	Assistant General Freight Agent
Agt.	Agent
Ala.	Alabama
Ald.	Alderman
Alt.	Altitude; alto
A. M.	(Ante Meridiem) Before noon
A. M. or M. A.	Master of Arts
Am., Amer.	American
Amt.	Amount
Anon.	Anonymous

Ans. or A.	Answer
Apr. or Apl.	April
Ariz.	Arizona
Ark.	Arkansas
Art.	Article
Assoc., Assn.	Association
Asst.	Assistant
Atty.	Attorney
Atty. Gen.	Attorney General
Aug.	August
A. V. or Auth. Ver.	Authorized Version
Ave. or Av.	Avenue
A-1	First class
@	At
b.	born
B. A.	Bachelor of Arts; British America
Bal.	Balance
Bart.	Baronet
Bbl.	Barrel
B. C.	Before Christ; British Columbia
B/C	Bales of Cotton
B/E	Bill of Exchange
Bet.	Between
B/L	Bill of Lading
B. L.	Bachelor of Laws
Bldg.	Building
Bor.	Borough
Bot.	Bought
Boul.	Boulevard
Bp.	Bishop
B/P	Bills Payable
B/R	Bills Receivable
Brig.-Gen.	Brigadier-General
Bros.	Brothers

B/S	Bill of Sale
Bu.	Bushel
B. V.	(Beata Virgo) Blessed Virgin
C.	(Centum) Hundred
C. A.	Chartered Accountant
C. a. f.	Cost and freight
Cal. or Calif.	California
Can.	Canada
Capt.	Captain
Cash.	Cashier
Cat.	Catalogue
Cath.	Catholic
C. C.	County Court; County Clerk
C. C. P.	Court of Common Pleas
C. E.	Civil Engineer
Cent., Ct.	(Centum) Hundred
Cert., Ctf., Certif.	Certificate
Chap., Ch. or c.	Chapter
Chgd.	Charged
C. i. f.	Cost, insurance and freight
C. J., Ch. J.	Chief Justice
Ck.	Check
c/o	Care of
Co.	Company; county
C. O. D.	Cash or Collect on Delivery
Col.	Colonel; college
Coll.	Collector
Colo. or Col.	Colorado
Com.	Common; Commodore; Committee; Commission
Com. Arr.	Committee of Arrangements
Comr.	Commissioner
Com. Ver.	Common Version
Cong.	Congress; congregation

Conj.	Conjunction
Conn., Ct.	Connecticut
Consol., Cons.	Consolidated
Const.	Constable; Constitution
Contr.	Contract; contractor; contraction
Copr.	Copyright
Cor.	Coroner; Corinthians; corner
Corp.	Corporation
Cor. Sec.	Corresponding Secretary
C. P.	Common Pleas; Court of Probate; Candle Power
C. P. A.	Certified Public Accountant
Cr.	Credit; creditor
Cresc.	(Crescendos—Music) Louder
C. S.	Civil Service
C. S. A.	Confederate States of America
Cts., ¢	Cents
Cu.	Cubic
C. w. o.	Cash with order
Cwt.	Hundredweight
d.	Penny; died
D. A. R.	Daughters of the American Revolution
D. C.	District of Columbia
D. C. L.	Doctor of Civil Law
D/d	Days' date
D. D.	Doctor of Divinity
D. D. S.	Doctor Dental Surgery
Dec.	Deceased; December
Deft., Def., Dft.	Defendant
Deg.	Degree
Del.	Delaware
Dem.	Democratic
Dept.	Department

D. F.	Defender of the Faith
Dft.	Draft; defendant
D. H.	Dead Head
Dict.	Dictated; dictator
Dim.	(Diminuendo—Music) Softer
Dis., disc.	Discount
Dist.	District
Dist. Atty.	District Attorney
Div.	Dividend; division
D. Lit.	Doctor of Literature
D. L. O.	Dead Letter Office
Do.	Ditto—the same
Dol.	Dollar
Doz.	Dozen
D. P.	Doctor of Philosophy
Dr.	Debit; debtor; Doctor; drachm
D/S	Days' sight
D. T.	Delirium tremens
D. V.	(Deo volente) God willing
dwt.	pennyweight
E.	East
Ea.	Each
E. C.	East Center (London Postal District)
Eccl.	Ecclesiastes
Econ.	Economics
Ed.	Editor; edition
E. E.	Errors excepted; electrical engineer
e. g.	(exempli gratia) For example
Elec.	Electric; Electricity
Enc.	Enclosure; enclosed
Eng.	England
e. r.	en route (on the way)
Esq.	Esquire

Est.	Estimated; Estate
Estab.	Established
et al.	(et alii) And others
Etc.	(et cetera) And other things; &c. And so forth
Ex.	Example; exodus; exception
Exch.	Exchange
Ex. Com.	Executive Committee
Exec.	Executor
Exp.	Expense; express; export
Extrx.	Executrix
E. & O. E.	Errors and Omissions Excepted
F., Fahr.	Fahrenheit (thermometer)
Feb.	February
Fem.	Feminine
ff.	(Fortissimo—Music) Very loud
Fin. Com.	Finance Committee
Fin. Sec.	Financial Secretary
Fla.	Florida
F. O. B.	Free on Board
Fol.	Folio (ff-folios); following
For'd	Forward
F. P.	Fire Plug
Fri.	Friday
Frs.	Francs
Frt.	Freight
Ft.	Feet; 12′ (12 feet); Fort
Fut.	Futures
Ga.	Georgia
G. A.	General Agent
Gal.	Gallon
G. A. R	Grand Army of the Republic
G. B.	Great Britain
G. C. A.	General Claim Agent

Gen.	General
Gen. Del.	General Delivery
G. F. A.	General Freight Agent
Gov.	Governor; Government
Gov. Gen.	Governor General
G. P. A.	General Passenger Agent
G. P. O.	General Post Office
Gr.	Grain; gross
Hab. corp.	(Habeas Corpus) Produce the body
H. B. M.	His or Her Britannic Majesty
Hdkf.	Handkerchief
H. E.	His Excellency; His Eminence
Heb.	Hebrew
Hf.	Half
Hhd.	Hogshead
H. I.	Hawaiian Islands
H. I. H.	His or Her Imperial Highness
H. I. M.	His or Her Imperial Majesty
H. M. S.	His or Her Majesty's Service or Ship
Hon.	Honorable; honorary
Hon. Sec.	Honorary Secretary
Hor.	Horizon
Hort.	Horticulturist
H. P.	Horse Power
H. R.	House of Representatives
Ia.	Iowa
Ib. or ibid.	(Ibidem) In the same place
Id.	(Idem) The same
Ida.	Idaho
i. e.	(id est) that is
I. H. N.	In His Name
I. H. S.	(Iesus Hominum Salvator) Jesus the Savior of Men

Ill., or Ills.	Illinois
Illus., Illust.	Illustration
In. (″)	Inch, 12″ (12 inches)
Inc.	Incorporated; increase
Incl.	Including; inclusive
Incog.	Incognito (Unknown)
Ind.	Indiana
I. N. R. I.	(Iesus Nazarenus Rex Indaerum) Jesus of Nazareth, King of the Jews
Ins.	Insurance; inspector
Inst.	(Instant) Present month; institution
Int.	Interest
Inv.	Invoice
Invt.	Inventory
I. O. O. F.	Independent Order of Odd Fellows
I. O. U.	I Owe You
Itin.	Itinerary
It., Ital.	Italics
I. W. W.	Industrial Workers of the World
J.	Justice; JJ. Justices
Jan.	January
Jour.	Journal
J. P.	Justice of the Peace
Jr.	Junior
Kan., Kans.	Kansas
K. C.	Knights of Columbus
Kilo., Kilog.	Kilogram
Kilom.	Kilometer
K. W.	Kilowatt
Ky.	Kentucky
L. or £	(Libra) Pound in English money
La., Lou.	Louisiana
Lat.	Latitude

Lb.	Pound (weight)
L. C.	Letter of Credit
Ledg.	Ledger
leg.	(Legato—Music) Smoothly
L. I.	Long Island
Lib., Libr.	Librarian; liber (book)
Lieut.	Lieutenant
Lieut. Col.	Lieutenant Colonel
Lim., Ltd.	Limited
Litt. D.	Doctor of Literature
L.L. A.	A woman literate in arts
LL. B.	Bachelor of Laws
LL. D.	Doctor of Laws
Long.	Longitude
L. S.	(Locus sigilli) Place of the seal
£. s. d.	Pounds, shilling, pence
LXX	(Septuagint Version) Old Greek Version
M.	Noon; Monsieur; thousand; mile; minute
Mach.	Machinery
Maj.	Major
Mar., Mch.	March
Masc.	Masculine
Mass.	Massachusetts
M. C.	Member of Congress
Md.	Maryland
M. D.	Doctor of Medicine
Mdlle., Mlle.	Madamoiselle
Mdm.	Madam
Mdse.	Merchandise
Me.	Maine
M. E.	Methodist Episcopal; Mining Engineer Mechanical Engineer

Meas.	Measure
Memo., Mem.	Memorandum
Messrs., MM.	Messieurs
Mex.	Mexico
mf.	(Mezzo forte—Music) Moderately loud
Mfg.	Manufacturing
Mfrs.	Manufacturers
Mgr.	Manager; Monsignor
Mich.	Michigan
Min.	Minute; mining
Minn.	Minnesota
Miscl., Misc.	Miscellaneous
Miss.	Mississippi
Mlle., Mdlle.	Mademoiselle
Mme.	Madame
Mmes.	Mesdames
Mo.	Missouri; month
Mon.	Monday; Monsignor (also Monsig. —Mgr.)
Mont.	Montana
M. P.	Member of Parliament
Mr.	Mister
Mrs.	Mistress
MS.	Manuscript (plural MSS.)
N.	North
N. A.	North America; National Academy
N. A. O. W. S.	National Association Opposed to Woman Suffrage
Natl., Nat.	National
Naut.	Nautical
N. B.	(Nota Bene) Note well; New Brunswick
N. C.	North Carolina

N. D. or N. Dak.	North Dakota
N. E.	New England; North East
Nebr., Neb.	Nebraska
Nev.	Nevada
N. F.	Newfoundland
N. G.	No good; National Guard
N. H.	New Hampshire
N. J.	New Jersey
N. M., N. Mex.	New Mexico
No.	Number
Nov.	November
N. P.	Notary Public
N. S.	Nova Scotia
N. T.	New Testament
N. W. S. A.	National Woman Suffrage Association
N. Y.	New York
O.	Ohio
Obs.	Obsolete
Oct.	October
O. K.	All right
Okla.	Oklahoma
Ont.	Ontario
Opp.	Opposite
Ore., Org., Or.	Oregon
Orig.	Original
oz.	ounce
p.	piano; page
P. A.	Purchasing Agent; Power of Attorney
Par.	Paragraph
Part.	Participle
Pcs.	Pieces
Pd.	Paid

Penn. or Pa.	Pennsylvania
Per an.	Per annum (by the year)
Per cent. or per ct. or %	Per centum (per hundred)
Pfd.	Preferred
Ph. D.	Doctor of Philosophy
P. I.	Philippine Islands
Pk.	Peck
Pl.	Plural
Pltf.	Plaintiff
P. M.	(Post Meridiem) After noon; Postmaster
P. M. G.	Postmaster General
P. O.	Post Office
Pop.	Population
pp.	(Pianissimo—Music) Very softly; pages
P. P.	Per Procuration
P. P. C.	(Pour Prendre Conge) to take leave; Pullman Parlor Car
Pr.	Pair
Prem.	Premium
Pres.	President
Pri. Sec.	Private Secretary
Prin.	Principal
Prof.	Professor
Prot.	Protestant
Pro tem.	(Pro tempore) For the time being
Prox.	(Proximo) Next month
P. S.	(Post scriptum) Postscript; Public Service; Public School
P. T.	Paying Teller
Pt.	Pint
Pub.	Publisher; public

Pwt.	Pennyweight
Q.	Query; Question
Q. M.	Quartermaster
Qt.	Quart
Quar.	Quarterly
R.	Rods
℞	(recipe—prescription) Take
R. A.	Royal Academy; Royal Artillery; Russian-American
rall.	(Rallentando—Music) More slowly
R. C.	Roman Catholic; Red Cross
Recd.	Received
Rec. Sec.	Recording Secretary
Rect.	Receipt
Ref.	Reference
Reg.	Registered; Register
Regt.	Regiment
Rep.	Representative; Republican
Rev.	Reverend
R. F. D.	Rural Free Delivery
R. I.	Rhode Island
R. I. P.	(Requiescat in Pace) May he rest in peace
R. R.	Railroad
R/R	Respectfully Referred
R. S. V. P.	(Respondez s'il vous plait) Reply if you please
Rt. Hon.	Right Honorable
R. T., Rec. Tel.	Receiving Teller
Rt. Rev.	Right Reverend
R. V.	Revised Version
S.	Saint (plural SS.); South; Shilling
S. A.	South America
Sat.	Saturday

S. C.	South Carolina
S. cap.	Small capitals
S. D. or S. Dak.	South Dakota
S/D	Sight Draft
Sec.	Secretary; Section; Second
Sen.	Senate; Senator
Sept.	September
Serg.	Sergeant
Sgd.	Signed
Shs.	Shares
Sig.	Signor
S. J.	Society of Jesus (Jesuit Order)
S. O.	Seller's Option
Soc.	Society
S. O. S.	Wireless Signal of Distress
Sq.	Square
Sr.	Senior; Sister
S. S.	Steamship; Sunday School
ss.	(scilicet) It is permitted to know
St.	Street; Saint
Ster.	Sterling
Sun.	Sunday
Supt.	Superintendent
Surg.	Surgeon
T. A.	Traffic Agent; Travelling Agent
Tech.	Technology; technically
Tenn.	Tennessee
Tex.	Texas
Thurs.	Thursday
Tr.	Transpose; Trustee
Transf.	Transferred
Treas.	Treasurer
U.	Utah

U. D. C.	United Daughters of the Confederacy
Ult.	(Ultimo) Last month
Univ.	University
Unm.	Unmarried
U. S.	United States
U. S. A.	United States Army; United States of America
U. S. M.	United States Mail
U. S. N.	United States Navy
Ux.	(Uxor) Wife
v. or vs.	(Versus) Against
Va.	Virginia
Val.	Value
Var.	Varas (Texas, Mex., N. Mex., Ariz. and Cal. land measure)
V. C.	Victoria Cross; Vice Chancellor
Vid.	(Vide) See
Viz.	(Videlicet) To wit, namely
Vol.	Volume
V. P., Vice Pres.	Vice President
V. S.	Veterinary Surgeon
Vt.	Vermont
W.	West
Wash.	Washington
W. B. A.	Women Bankers' Association
W. C.	West Center (London Postal District)
W. C. T. U.	Women's Christian Temperance Union
Wed.	Wednesday
w. f.	wrong font
Wis.	Wisconsin
W. P. U.	Women's Political Union

Wt.	Weight
W. Va.	West Virginia
Wyo.	Wyoming
Xcp.	Ex-coupon
Xd.	Ex-dividend
Xi.	Ex-interest
Xmas.	Christmas
Yd.	Yard
Yr.	Year
Y. W. C. A.	Young Women's Christian Association

Abstract of Title. A summary of the instruments that go to prove the title to, or ownership in, a property; e.g., deeds, mortgages, judgments, mechanics liens, etc., etc.

Accident or Casualty Insurance. Insurance covering personal injury or accidents to travelers.

Acknowledgment. A formal declaration or admission before a Notary Public, or other officer duly authorized by the state, that a person has of his or her own free will executed a deed or other instrument. The forms vary for the different states.

NEW YORK FORM.

STATE OF.......................... ⎫
 ⎬ ss.:
COUNTY OF...................... ⎭

On this.....................day of.............................
in the year one thousand nine hundred and........before me personally

came and appeared..
to me known and known to me to be..............................
the person described in and who executed the foregoing instrument and
...................acknowledged to me that ...he executed the same.

....
Notary Public.

....
County.

In some states, when a married woman joins in a deed with her husband, it is usual to take her acknowledgment separate and apart from her husband with her statement that she is not being coerced by him but is signing of her own free will, viz:.

STATE OF..........................
ss.:
COUNTY OF.......................

*Be it remembered that on this..........day of.....................
in the year.................................before me...............
a Notary Public of the State of....................personally appeared
....
who I am satisfied are the.......................in the within.........
.....................; and I having first made known to them the
contents thereof they did acknowledge that they signed, sealed and
delivered the same as their voluntary act and deed, for the uses and
purposes therein expressed. And the said.........................
being by me privately examined, separate and apart from her said husband, did further acknowledge that she signed, sealed and delivered the
same as her voluntary act and deed, FREELY, without any fear, threats,
or compulsion of her said husband.*

.....................................(Notary Public)

While the lack of an acknowledgment does not invalidate a deed, it is necessary when the deed is to be recorded See *Deeds.*

18

Additions and Betterments. A railroad term meaning the improvements that enhance the value of the railroad property.

Ad Infinitum. And so on indefinitely.

Ad Litem. For the purpose of the suit.

Administrator. A person appointed by the court to distribute the property of a decedent who left no will. The next of kin is usually selected. (Feminine, Administratrix.) See *Letters of Administration* and *Wills*.

Affidavit. A declaration in writing affirmed and sworn to before an official duly authorized to administer oaths.

FORM OF AFFIDAVIT.

STATE OF..........................

COUNTY OF......................
} *ss.*:

....*being duly sworn says that* ....

....

....

....

....

Sworn to before me this

.............*day of*....................19 .

(*Sgd*)...

....

Notary Public No.

................*County.*

Agreement. A contract or covenant among two or more parties.

GENERAL FORM OF AGREEMENT.

This Agreement, *made the..................day of................
one thousand nine hundred and.............................between
................................of the city of........................
in the county of....................and state of....................
of the first part and......................................
of......................in said county and state, of the second part,*

Witnesseth, *that the said......................
in consideration of the covenants on the part of the party of the second
part, doth covenant and agree to and with the said....................
that (etc.).*

In Witness Whereof, *we have hereunto set our hands and seals,
the day and year first above written.*

Sealed and Delivered in the Presence of
   (2 *witnesses*)

             ....(L. S.)

             ....(L. S.)

Alias. An assumed name.

Alibi. Claim of the accused that he was in another place when the offense or act was committed.

Amortization. (Finance) The wiping out of a debt, as by a sinking fund. Any payment made toward such extinction. The accumulation of funds.

Annuity. Annual payment.

Appraise. To estimate or place a value upon.

Arbitage. Securities bought on one exchange or market and sold on another.

Assets and Liabilities. ASSETS—Property of every nature, real or personal, to which value may be attached, belonging to a person, estate, business or corporation, that may be used for the purpose of satisfying debts. Resources. "Liquid" assets are those that are readily turned into cash.

LIABILITIES—All debts and obligations.

"Current" assets and liabilities are those that change from time to time.

Assignment. The act of making over to another the right one has in a property. The instrument, under seal, duly witnessed, under which certain property rights are "granted, bargained, sold, assigned, transferred or set over" to another.

FORM OF ASSIGNMENT OF MORTGAGE.

Know All Men by These Presents, *That.....................
hereinafter designated as the party of the first part, for and in consideration of the sum of..............................Dollars, lawful money of the United States, to........in hand paid by..............
hereinafter designated as the party of the second part, at or before the ensealing and delivery of these presents, the receipt whereof is hereby acknowledged, has granted, bargained, sold, assigned, transferred and set over, and by these presents does grant, bargain, sell, assign, transfer and set over to the said party of the second part,......................
a certain indenture of mortgage given to secure payment of the sum of
.................................dollars and interest, bearing date the
........day of.................one thousand...............hundred
and........................ made by ....
to ....
and........recorded in the office of the...............of the County of..............on the...............day of...................., 1..,
in liber......of Section.............of mortgages, page......which said mortgage covers premises...................................
which said premises are included in Block Number......in Section......
on the Land Map of the City of New York.*

Together with ....
*the bond or obligation described in said mortgage, and the moneys due
and to grow due thereon with the interest.* **To have and to hold**
*the same to the said party of the second part, and to the successors,
personal representatives and assigns of the said party of the second
part, forever, subject only to the proviso in the said indenture of
mortgage mentioned.* **And the said** *party of the first part does hereby
make, constitute and appoint the said party of the second part the true
and lawful attorney, irrevocable, of the party of the first part, in the
name of the party of the first part, or otherwise, but at the proper
costs and charges of the party of the second part, to have, use and take
all lawful ways and means for the recovery of the said money and
interest, and in case of payment to discharge the same as fully as the
party of the first part might or could do, if these presents were not made.*
In Witness Whereof, *the said party of the first part has*..........
.... *signed* ....
.....................*and sealed these presents*.....................
..............*this*..............*day of*.....................*191*...
In the presence of ....(L. s.)

FORM OF ASSIGNMENT (OR TRANSFER) OF STOCK.

For Value Received...
hereby assign and transfer unto...................................
.... *share(s)* ....
of the stock of..*COMPANY,
represented by the Certificate on the reverse hereof, and do hereby
appoint* .... *Attorney irrevocable,
to transfer the said stock on the books of the above named company, this*
..............*day of*........................*191*...
(Signed) ....

In Presence of
....
....

See *Bonds and Stocks.*

Bankruptcy. Default in the payment of debts. **Failure.**
Insolvency. Insufficient funds to meet liabilities. Liabilities over Assets.

The U. S. Bankruptcy Act of July 1, 1898, as amended
by Act of June 25, 1910, provides:

SEC. 4. WHO MAY BECOME BANKRUPTS.—(*a*) Any person except a municipal railroad, insurance or banking corporation shall be entitled to the benefits of this act as a voluntary bankrupt.

The bankruptcy of a corporation shall not release its officers, directors, or stockholders, as such, from any liability under the laws of a State or Territory or of the United States.

(*b*) Any natural person, except a wage-earner or a person engaged chiefly in farming or the tillage of the soil, any unincorporated company and any moneyed business, or commercial corporation, except a municipal railroad, insurance or banking corporation, owing debts to the amount of one thousand dollars or over, may be adjudged an involuntary bankrupt upon default or an impartial trial and shall be subject to the provisions and entitled to the benefits of this act.

SEC. 7. DUTIES OF BANKRUPTS.—(a) The bankrupt shall (1) attend the first meeting of his creditors, if directed by the court or a Judge thereof to do so, and the hearing upon his application for a discharge, if filed; (2) comply with all lawful orders of the court; (3) examine the correctness of all proofs of claims filed against his estate; (4) execute and deliver such papers as shall be ordered by the court; (5) execute to his trustee transfers of all his property in foreign countries; (6) immediately inform his trustee of any attempt, by his creditors or other persons, to evade the provisions of this act, coming to his knowledge; (7) in case of any person having to his knowledge proved a false claim ⋅ against his estate, disclose that fact immediately to his trustee; (8) prepare, make oath to, and file in court within ten days, unless further time is granted, after the adjudication if an involuntary bankrupt, and with the petition if a voluntary bankrupt, a schedule of his property, showing the amount and kind of property, the location thereof, its money value in detail, and a list of his creditors, showing their residences, if known (if unknown that fact to be stated), the amount due each of them, the consideration thereof, the security held by them, if any, and a claim for such exemptions as he may be entitled to, all in triplicate, one copy of each for the clerk, one for the referee, and one for the trustee; and (9) when present at the first meeting of his creditors, and at such other times as the court shall order, submit to an examination concerning the conducting of his business, the cause of his bankruptcy, his dealings with his creditors and other persons, the amount, kind, and whereabouts of his property, and, in addition, all matters which may affect the administration and settlement of his estate; but no testimony given by him shall be offered in evidence against him in any criminal proceedings.

Provided, however, that he shall not be required to attend a meeting of his creditors, or at or for an examination at a place more than one hundred and fifty miles distant from his home or principal place of business, or to examine claims except when presented to him, unless ordered by the court, or a Judge thereof, for cause shown, and the bankrupt shall be paid his actual expenses from the estate when examined or required to attend at any place other than the city, town, or village of his residence.

Act of March 3, 1911 (Judicial Code) 36 Stat. 1134, as follows:

SEC. 24. Original jurisdiction in district courts.

"SEC. 130. The Circuit Courts of Appeals shall have the appellate and supervisory jurisdiction conferred upon them by the act entitled 'An act to establish a uniform system of bankruptcy throughout the United States,' approved July first, eighteen hundred and ninety-eight, and all laws amendatory thereof, and shall exercise the same in the manner therein prescribed."

SEC. 252 states the appellate jurisdiction of the Supreme Court conferred upon it by the Bankruptcy act of July 1, 1898.—(*World Almanac.*)

Bill.   An account rendered for services or amounts due.   A list of purchases with their prices.

NEW YORK, June 1, 1916

M R. B. W. LEECH

439 Black Street

TO **ENOCH WARD,** DR.
1132 NASSAU STREET

SERVICES In investigating the financial condition of the Terminal Dock Company...............		**$10,000.00**
DISBURSEMENTS:		
Railroad fare	$100.00	
Telegrams.....	8.00	
Printing......	200.00	
Miscl........	180.00	488.00
		$10,488.00

Received payment

FORM OF BILL FOR SERVICES.

```
                              Feb. 1,
              NEW YORK,..................1916
MR. JOHN SMITH
..........................................................
              725 Main Street
..........................................................
         To L. W. MORRIS, DR.
            40 NASSAU STREET
```

Jan.	26	1 box Emb. Note Paper		60		
	29	1 Inkwell Cover		20		80

FORM OF BILL FOR SUPPLIES.

Bill of Lading. A receipt for merchandise issued by a steamship company, a railroad or other carrier to the shipper, acknowledging receipt of the goods from the shipper and agreeing to deliver them safely to consignee. One copy of the Bill of Lading is kept by the shipper, one by the carrier (consignor) and one is sent to the consignee. A Bill of Lading may be assigned.

FORM OF BILL OF LADING.

Contract No..........

Received *for shipment, in apparent good order and condition, from ....to be transported by the Steamer ....or other A1 Steamers, to sail from the port of ....and bound for.... ....(or so near thereto as she may safely get and always lie afloat), having liberty to call at intermediate ports or any port or ports in or out of the customary route, in any order, to receive and/or discharge coal, cargo, pas-*

sengers, and for any other purposes,...............................
...
said to weigh.............pounds, being marked and numbered as per
margin (quality, quantity, gauge, contents, weight and value unknown),
and to be delivered in like good order and condition from the vessel's
rail (where carrier's responsibility ceases) at the port of.............
unto order................................or to his or their assigns,
he or they paying freight in exchange for delivery order for said goods,
in cash without allowance for credit or discount, in the usual money of
the country where vessel discharges; settlement to be made on the basis
of 4 Shillings and 2 Pence, 4.30 Marks, 5.35 Francs, 2.55 Dutch Guilders,
3.80 Kroners, 5.35 Lire Gold to the United States Dollar, or at the
option of the consignee, settlement to be made at the rate of $4.80 to the
pound sterling at the current rate of exchange officially quoted on the
day the steamer enters the Custom House at port of discharge, for which
bankers' demand bills on London can be bought; (any custom or law of
the port of discharge to the contrary notwithstanding), at the rate of
................................cents United States Gold Currency,
per one hundred pounds (100 pounds) on the actual gross invoice or
discharged weight at vessel's option, charges as per margin and average
accustomed. Consignees shall exhibit the true invoice to vessel's agent
whenever called upon to do so.

IN WITNESS WHEREOF, *the Master or Agent of said vessel hath affirmed to this ONE Bill of Lading, which being accomplished shall be given up to the carrier and stand void.*

Bill of Exchange. An unconditional order in writing addressed by one person (the drawer) to the debtor (the drawee), signed by the drawer, requiring the drawee, or person to whom it is addressed, to pay the sum specified on demand, or to the bearer. Some Bills of Exchange are payable in 30, 60 or 90 days. A Bill of Exchange may be endorsed and is negotiable. When the drawee accepts the Bill of Exchange for payment, he then becomes the "acceptor." Checks and Drafts are Bills of Exchange.

FORM OF BILL OF EXCHANGE.

Bill of Sale. An instrument (not necessarily under seal) by which one person conveys to another a number of articles, or the right, title and interest in personal property. An assignment of goods and chattels.

FORM OF BILL OF SALE.

𝕂now all 𝕄en by these 𝕡resents, *That* ....
....
of the first part, for and in consideration of the sum of...............
....*lawful money of the United States,*

to....................*in hand paid, at or before the ensealing and delivery of these presents, by..*
of the second part, the receipt whereof is hereby acknowledged, ha...
bargained and sold, and by these presents do grant and convey, unto
the said part........of the second part,........executors, administrators and assigns,

(Here insert property)

To have and to hold *the same unto the said part....of the second part, ...executors, administrators and assigns forever. And......do......for......heirs, executors and administrators, covenant and agree to and with the said part......of the second part, to warrant and defend the sale of the said.....................hereby sold unto the said part......of the second part,......executors, administrators and assigns against all and every person and persons whomsoever.*

In Witness Whereof,.....*have hereunto set.......hand and seal.. the.................day of...................in the year one thousand nine hundred and...*

Signed, Sealed and Delivered in the presence of

Bimetallism.	Double standard of currency—gold and silver. The single standard is known as monometallism.
Board of Trade.	Association of business men to develop and protect the trade of a town or city.
Bona Fide.	In good faith. MALA FIDE, not in good faith.
Bonanza.	Gold mine. Highly speculative enterprise.
Bonds and Stock.	BONDS—Instruments by which a government, municipality or corporation contracts and agrees to pay a specified sum of money

on a given date, the bond itself being a coupon-bearing (or registered) note under seal; the coupons representing quarterly, semi-annual or annual interest at a fixed rate; a *"registered"* bond is one that is registered on the books of a company against loss, has the name of the owner filled out on the face, cannot be transferred from one person to another without endorsement upon the back by the party in whose name it is registered and sending to some designated office for transfer.

STOCK—Represents money contributed by individuals for the conduct of a business. PREFERRED STOCK is that stock which has a claim upon the property and earnings of a corporation prior to some other stock. COMMON STOCK is that part of the capitalization of a company upon which dividends may be paid only after satisfying the requirements of the floating debt, bonds and preferred stock; usually represents a "speculative" ownership in a corporation. —(*Extract from "Municipal and Corporation Bonds" by Montgomery Rollins.*)

A share of stock may be transferred or sold to another by filling out the blank form of transfer on the back of the certificate (see *Assignment of Stock*); but the new owner has no right to vote as a stockholder or receive dividends unless and until the certificate of stock has been turned in to the company and his name registered on the books of the company. If the stock is loaned or hypothecated the owner cannot vote.

"Watered" stock means that the shares of a stock company have been increased to a much greater extent than the amount of capital actually paid in.

```
INCORPORATED UNDER THE LAWS OF THE
          STATE OF NEW YORK
NUMBER 1498                              SHARES 25

      BIGLOW RUBBER COMPANY
          CAPITAL STOCK, $1,000,000.

This Certifies that Mark Regan is the owner of Twenty-
five Shares of the Capital Stock of
          BIGLOW RUBBER COMPANY
transferable only on the books of the Corporation by the holder hereof in person
or by Attorney upon surrender of this Certificate properly endorsed.
    In Witness Whereof, the said Corporation has caused this Certificate
to be signed by its duly authorized officers and to be sealed with the seal of the
          Corporation this 2nd day of November, 1914.

( SEAL )    ----------------------    ----------------------
                 Treasurer                  President
            SHARES, $10 EACH
```

FORM OF CERTIFICATE OF STOCK.

Bond of Indemnity.   See *Surety*.

Bonus.   An additional or gratuitous amount given for a loan, privilege, or as an extra dividend or stock to shareholders in a company; a premium; surplus.

Bourse.   A place where merchants and bankers meet for the transaction of business. Paris stock exchange.   See *Stock Exchange*.

Bradstreet.   Publisher of commercial ratings.

Bucketshop.   An office where gambling or pretended trading in the stocks listed on the larger exchanges is carried on, no actual deliveries being made.

Building and Loan Association. Building and loan associations—or, as they they are officially known in New York State, savings and loan associations—are mutual associations of home-builders, who admit, both from their own ranks and from outsiders, savings members, that is, those who buy stock. The vast majority of these co-operative associations naturally confine their loans to a restricted territory, often only one section of a city, known to the officers. Responsible persons who have bought a lot and paid for it in full are lent funds on first mortgage to build a home, the loan being repayable in monthly instalments. The funds come from the savings members who buy shares, usually paying $1 per share down and $1 a month. These shares can be withdrawn, either on demand or upon one or two months' notice; but the profits are larger if they are allowed to remain. Dividends are not paid every three or six months or yearly upon these shares as upon corporation stock; but, as profits from lending money accumulate, they are applied to the balance due on shares, and the investor at the end of a few years receives his share fully paid for, usually $100 or $200.

A distinctive feature of these associations is that the management is not remunerated, and the safety of shares depends upon knowing that the officers are men of integrity and good judgment as to the value of local real estate and the ability of the home-builders to pay their instalments.

From the very nature of the case, information regarding these associations must be obtained from local sources or from the State departments that usually have charge of them. In many States, including Wisconsin, the banking commissioner has full charge. The Banking Department of New York reports that in 1912 expenses of conducting the local associations was but 74 cents for each $100 of invested capital, while the dividend averaged 5 6-10 per cent.—(*From McClure's Magazine, "Your Money and How to Make it Earn."*)

Bulls and Bears. The terms "Bulls" and "Bears" are customarily accepted to mean as follows: "Bull": one who believes that higher prices will prevail and buys stock or commodities accordingly; presumably originating in the characteristic of the animal to toss up. "Bear": one who believes that lower prices will prevail and sells stock or commodities accordingly; the name presumably originating in the characteristic of the animal to tear down.

Business Laws. Ignorance of the law excuses no one. Everyone is bound to know the law and cannot plead ignorance of it.

A receipt for money paid is not legally conclusive.

Every agreement must have a consideration expressed.

Notes obtained from minors, by fraud, or from intoxicated persons cannot be collected.

Unless otherwise specified, a note is considered payable on demand.

A check should be presented for payment as soon as possible.

Contracts made with a minor, lunatic, or on Sunday, are not binding.

Principals are responsible for the acts of their agents.

Each partner is responsible for the whole debts of the firm.

The act of one partner binds all the others.

It is a fraud to conceal a fraud.

Lead pencil signatures are considered good in law.

By-Laws. When a company is formed, a set of by-laws are framed, defining the rules under which the business shall be conducted, usually providing about as follows:

That the business of the company shall be managed by a board of directors, elected by the stockholders at their first annual meeting, who shall hold office until the following or next annual meeting; that every stockholder present at such meetings in person or by proxy is entitled to one vote for each share of stock he owns, provided no share of stock has been transferred on the books of the company or hypothecated; that a majority of the stockholders shall constitute a quorum; that the duties of the officers shall be as follows:

PRESIDENT—To preside at all meetings of the stockholders and all meetings of the Board of Directors, to sign all certificates of stock and bonds, all conveyances, etc., and have general control and management of the affairs of the Company.

VICE PRESIDENT—To act and perform all the duties of the President in his absence.

SECRETARY—To issue all certificates of stock and bonds,

attest same as Secretary and affix the seal of the Company thereto; provide and keep the necessary books, record minutes of stockholders' and directors' meetings, and perform such other duties as may be assigned to him by the President and Board of Directors.

TREASURER—To receive all money, safely keep the same, and pay it out, keeping full and accurate account of such receipts and disbursements. He shall give bond to the Company for the faithful performance of his duties.

Cablegrams. Divided into the following classes: PLAIN LANGUAGE, CODE AND CIPHER, FULL RATE, DEFERRED HALF RATE MESSAGES, CABLE LETTERS, AND WEEK-END LETTERS.

PLAIN LANGUAGE MESSAGES—Neither in code nor cipher. May be written in any language that can be expressed in Roman letters. Each word of fifteen letters or less is counted and charged as a word. Words of over fifteen letters are counted and charged for at the rate of fifteen letters or fractions of fifteen letters to a word.

Example: RESPONSIBILITY   14 letters 1 word
             UNCONSTITUTIONAL   16 letters 2 words

CODE MESSAGES—May contain words belonging to one or more of the following languages; English, French, German, Italian, Dutch, Portuguese, Spanish or Latin. Code messages may also contain artificial words, that is, groups of letters so combined as to be pronounceable in at least one of the eight admitted languages.

Example: OFFENSEFUL (code dictionary word)
10 letters—1 word

ABACABOBAN (artificial word)
10 letters—1 word

In code messages, each code word (whether genuine or artificial) of ten letters or less is counted and charged as one word. No code word of more than ten letters is accepted. If any words in plain language and of MORE than ten letters each are used in Code messages, they are counted at the rate of ten letters to a word.

CIPHER LANGUAGE—Formed of groups of figures or groups of letters having a secret meaning, each uninterrupted series being counted at the rate of five figures or five letters to a word.

Words in plain language inserted in such messages are counted and charged at the rate of fifteen letters or fraction thereof to the word.

Example: 19554 42768 RESPONSIBILITY (3 words)

xbqgr yhtwc UNCONSTITUTIONAL

(4 words)

Figures AND letters are counted separately.

Example: a5C—counted and charged as three words.

FULL RATE MESSAGES—Code or cipher permitted. Accepted for immediate transmission and delivery.

DEFERRED HALF RATE MESSAGES—Communications of a non-urgent character.

Must be written in plain language of the country of

origin or destination, or they may be written in French as a Universal language. The use of more than one language in the same message is not permitted.

The sender must write before the address, and *pay the charge on one word for* the letters LCO (language country of origin) or LCD (language country of destination) or LCF (language country French), according to the language in which the message is written.

Except in the address, all numbers should be spelled out.

Code or registered cable address may be used.

Subject to being deferred in favor of Full-Rate messages for not exceeding 19 to 24 hours.

Rate—one-half regular cable rate, except on messages destined to points in Great Britain and Ireland, when 3 cents per word less than half regular rates.

Any cablegram filed *without an indication* that it is to be sent as a Deferred Half Rate message is assumed to be intended for immediate transmission and is sent with full paid cablegrams.

CABLE LETTERS—For plain-language business and social communications, which it is not desired to subject to the over-sea mail's delay, yet which are not of sufficient urgency and importance to warrant payment of full cable tolls on the same. Are subject to transmission at the Telegraph Company's convenience and have a fixed time of delivery, well within 24 hours from time of filing.

Must be written in plain language of the country of origin, or the language of the country of destination.

Code language is not accepted, although code addresses may be used.

The use of more than one language in the same message is not permitted.

Rate—75 cents for 13 words (which includes the necessary indicator) and 5 cents for each additional word between New York, Boston, Halifax or Montreal and London or Liverpool, plus Night Letter rates to New York and regular charges beyond London if telegraphic delivery is desired.

WEEK-END LETTERS—Differ from Cable Letters only in the increased number of words included in the minimum charge, and in the time of delivery.

The minimum number of words charged for is 25.

May be filed before midnight Saturday for delivery Monday.

Must be written in plain language of country of origin or the language of the country of destination. Use of more than one language in the same message not permitted.

Code language not accepted, although the address may be coded.

Rate—$1.15 for 25 words (which includes the necessary indicator) and 5 cents for each additional word.

WIRELESS PREPAID MESSAGES—Accepted for transmission by Wireless at sender's risk to nearly all of the Atlantic and Pacific Ocean Steamships and boats on the Great Lakes and Long Island Sound.

GENERAL RULES FOR WRITING CABLEGRAMS.

Every message must be prepaid, unless otherwise specifically arranged.

All words in the address, text and signature are charged for.

In the address of any message, the name of the office of destination, the name of the country and the name of the territorial subdivisions are each charged as one word, no matter how many letters are employed.

Cable addresses may be registered free of charge with the Telegraph Company. Foreign Government Telegraphs charge for this service.

The address of every message must consist of at least two words, the first indicating the name of the receiver and the second the name of the office of destination.

Corrections or alterations must be made in a new cablegram, which must be paid for.

Every isolated figure, letter or character counts as one word.

Words joined by a hyphen or separated by an apostrophe are charged for as so many separate words. (Example, Navy-yard, 2 words).

Signs of punctuation, hyphens and apostrophes are not counted or sent except upon formal demand of the sender, in which case they will be charged for as one word each.

Inverted commas, the two signs of parenthesis, and each separate figure, letter, underline or character will be counted as one word.

When the letters "ch" come together in the spelling of a word, they are counted as one letter. (Example, "Chiropodist" 10 letters). In artificial words, however, the combination is counted as two letters.

The following examples determine the interpretation of the rules to be followed in counting words

| | Number of Words. | | | | Number of Words. | | |
| | In Address | Text | | | In Address | Text | |
		Plain Language Messages.	Code Language Messages.			Plain Language Messages.	Code Language Messages.
New York.........	1	2	2	444 55 (6 characters)		2	2
Newyork..........	1	1	1	44/2 (4 characters).		1	1
Frankfurt Main....	1	2	2	44/ (3 characters)..		1	1
Frankfurt a/M......	1	2	2	2% (4 characters)...		1	1
Frankfurtmain.....	1	1	2	2 p %.............		3	3
Sanct Poelten.....	1	2	2	54-58 (5 characters).		1	1
Sanctpoelten......	1	1	2	17me (4 characters).		1	1
Emmingen Hannover*.....	1	2	3	E................		1	1
Emmingen Wurttemburg*........	1	2	3	E M (isolated letters)...........		2	2
Newsouthwales	1	1	2	Emythf (6 characters)............		2	2
(R P 16) supplementary instructions written in abridged form)............	1			Ch23.............		2	2
				G H F 45.........		4	4
Vandebrando (name of a person)......		1	2	A5C..............		3	3
Du Bois...........		2	2	197a/199a........		4	4
Dubois (name of a person)..........		1	1	AP................		1	1
Belgrave Square....		2	2	Le 1529me (1 word and a group of 6 characters).......		3	3
Belgravesquare (contrary to the usage of the language)..		2	2	10 francs 50 centimes (or) 10 fr. 50 c.............		4	4
Hydepark (contrary to the usage of the language)........		2	2	10 fr. 50............		3	3
Hydepark Square‡..	2	2	2	Fr. 10.50............		2	2
Saint James Street..	3	3	3	11.30..............		1	1
Saintjames Street ..	2	2	2	huit /10............		2	2
Allright...........		2	2	5bis...............		2	2
Alright........		2	2	30a†..............		3	3
Rue de la Paix.....		4	4	15 x 6†............		4	4
Rue delapaix.......		2	2	Two hundred and thirty four		5	5
Responsibility......		1	2	Twohundredandthirtyfour (23 characters).......		2	3
Unconstitutionality (19 characters)...		2	2	Troisceuxriets......		1	2
A-t-il............		3	3	Unneufdixiemes.....		1	2
C'est-a-dire........		4	4	Deux mille cent quatre vingtquatroze..		6	6
Aujourd'hui........		2	2	Deuxmilecentquatrevingtquatroze (31 characters).......		3	4
Aujourdhui........		1	1	3/M }		2	2
Porte-monnaie......		2	2	(Private) the affair is urgent, leave at once (one pair of brackets, one underline).........		10	10
Portemonnaie.	1	1	2				
Prince of Wales (ship)	3	3	3				
Princeofwales (ship).	1	1	2				
44 1/2 (5 characters)		1	1				
4441/2 (6 characters)		2	2				
444.5 (5 characters)		1	1				

† Telegraph instruments cannot reproduce such expressions as 30a 15 x 6, etc. Senders must be asked to substitute for them the explicit meanings "30 exponant a," "15 multiplied by 6," etc.

* Hannover and Wurttemburg following Emmingen, serve to complete the designation of two offices of the same name in the same State, and thus appear in the first column of the official nomenclature of telegraph offices.

‡ In this case, the expression "Hydepark," written as a single word, counts as one word, because the work "park" forms an integral part of the name of the square.

Abbreviations, misspelled words, illegitimate compound words, words combined in a manner contrary to the usages of the several languages authorized, also unpronounceable groups of letters (not trademarks or marks of commerce) are inadmissable, but if they should accidentally appear in a message the unpronounceable groups will be charged for at the rate of five letters, or fractions of five letters, as one word, and the others in accordance with the number of words they actually contain.

Upon payment of a quarter of the full rate, in addition to the ordinary tolls, a cable message will be repeated, which ensures its correct transmission.

Repetition of a doubtful word or words may be requested by the addressee without charge by the Cable Co therefor.

Capital.   The amount of money put into a business. Available funds.

Capitaliza- See *Bonds and Stocks.*
tion.

Capital
Letters.
Begin with a capital:

    (1) The first word of every *complete* sentence, whether simple or compound.

> *Examples*: (Simple Sentence) Experience develops a stenographer.
>
> (Compound Sentence) One of the questions answered herein is: How shall I properly write a check?

(2) The first word of each line of poetry.

Examples:

I didn't begin with askings,
I took my job, and I stuck,
And I took the chance they wouldn't,
And now they're calling it "luck."

—*Kipling.*

(3) Proper nouns and words derived from proper nouns.

Examples: Engineer Lee, ex-President Roosevelt, Grace, Riverside Drive, Chicago, War of 1812, New Thought, Professor Jones, President Blank, Good Queen Bess, King George, Roman, Ohio, Victorian, Interstate Commerce Commission, Brigadier-General.

(4) Words used to indicate the Deity.

Examples: He, Him, Thou, Thy, Thee, Heaven, Providence, God, Father, Son, Holy Ghost, Supreme Being, the Almighty, etc.

God indicating a heathen deity is not capitalized. "Thou shalt have no other gods before me."

Heavens (plural), when the sky is meant, is not capitalized.

(5) Names of things personified.

Examples:

"O Death, where is thy sting."
"The Sea saw it and fled."

(6) Months of the year, days of the week, and holidays.

Examples: January, Monday, Lincoln's Birthday.

Names of the seasons (spring, summer, autumn and winter) are not capitalized. When autumn is referred to as "the Fall," *Fall* is begun with a capital letter.

(7)   The first words of a *direct* quotation.

> *Examples*:   The Oliver Typewriter Company replied: "To make the pound Sterling mark, strike a small *f* over a small *t*."
>
> (*Indirect Quotation*): The Oliver Typewriter Company replied that the pound Sterling mark could be made "by striking the hyphen over the capital *L*," if we did not wish to make the sign with ink.

(8)   The words *north, south, east* and *west,* when indicating a section of the country and not direction.

> *Examples*:
> This interesting story comes from the West.
> The wind is from the east.

(9)   Personal pronoun *I* and interjection *O.*

The interjection *oh* is not capitalized except at the beginning of a sentence; and is always followed by a comma or an exclamation-mark. "The stamp—oh! I forgot to put it on."

The interjection *O* seldom has a punctuation-mark after it, as, "O Miss Smith, this is not the letter."

(10)   Important words in the title of a book, picture, play, heading, subject of a chapter, article or

paragraph.   (Each noun, verb, adjective, and adverb.)

> *Examples*: The title of this book is, "What Every Business Woman Should Know."
>
> "The Roman Girl at the Well," "The Girl of the Golden West."
>
> Car Demurrage and Freight Revenue, Article I, Resolved, Whereas.

When jointly used with proper names, or when indicating that the person is directly addressed, *mother, father, sister, brother, cousin, aunt, etc.* are capitalized.

> *Examples*
>
> "I agree with you, Mother, it is the better way."
> Aunt Mary, Cousin Margaret, Sister Sue.
> My uncle and aunt are en route to California.

The names of articles or goods, or terms that are peculiar to a certain line of business, are frequently capitalized.

The prefix *ex* is not capitalized except at the beginning of a sentence.

> *Example*: Among those present were ex-Judge Townes and ex-President Taft.

In typewriting, either capitals or small letters may be used for a.m. and p.m.; as, *10:30 P.M., 9 a.m.* There should be no space between the two letters.

Care of Important Papers. Every reasonable precaution should be taken against loss of important papers, either by theft, fire or whatever the case may be, and no better precaution can be taken than by renting a box in some safe deposit company. There is no recorded instance of an effort to break into a modern safe deposit vault. The physical obstacles offered by the construction are too great. There are a great many people who think they cannot afford a deposit box, but in the long run it proves a very cheap method of insurance. Have a complete list of the papers to be preserved made, and keep this in a SEPARATE place from where the actual documents are kept, in an entirely different building if possible, so that if the papers are destroyed by fire the same fire will not destroy the list. —(*From "Municipal and Corporation Bonds" by Montgomery Rollins.*)

Casualty Insurance. See *Accident or Casualty Insurance.*

Caveat. An order to hold action on the specified matter in abeyance until further notice or advice is received, e. g., a caveat may be filed against the probate of a will.

Certificate of Deposit. A certificate issued against a deposit of money, payable at a fixed due date determined by the depositor. Interest is allowed at a rate which depends on the amount of the deposit and the length of time for which the certificate is issued. Checks cannot be issued against these funds.

44

```
┌─────────────────────────────────────────────────────────┐
│          │  First National Bank of Statetown             │
│ CERTIFICATE OF DEPOSIT │                                 │
│ NOT SUBJECT TO CHECK   │ No.        Statetown,——————19——— │
│          │ ——————————————————————ha—— deposited in this  │
│          │ Bank——————————————————————————————Dollars     │
│          │ payable to the order of—————————————————————   │
│          │ upon the return of this Certificate properly endorsed, with interest │
│          │ at————— per cent. per annum if left—————————————months. │
│          │ PAYMENT SUBJECT TO TWO WEEKS NOTICE.          │
│          │                                                │
│          │        ————————————————————————Cashier.        │
│          │ $—————————————                                 │
└─────────────────────────────────────────────────────────┘
```

FORM OF CERTIFICATE OF DEPOSIT.

Certiorari. A writ removing an action from a lower to a higher court.

Chamber of Commerce. Association of business men to develop and protect the trade of a town or city.

Charter. The grant of certain powers or privileges to a company or corporation.

Charter Party. The contract or instrument embodying the terms under which a ship is hired. A mercantile lease of a ship.

FORM OF CHARTER PARTY.

*Articles of Agreement, made this............day of............
by and between........................of the city of...............
party of the first part, and..................................
of the same place, party of the second part,*

Witnesseth, that the said party of the first part has this day chartered and hired unto the said party of the second part the vessel named ....of..................and of the burden of.........

*tons, or thereabouts, with all the appurtenances, cables, anchors, chains,
etc., which belong to said vessel, for the term of..............months,
from the...........day of...................., to be delivered at the
port of..................*

For the use *of said vessel the said party of the second part agrees
and binds himself to pay to the said party of the first part the sum of
.................................dollars, the payment to be made as
follows:....................dollars on the delivery of said vessel;
....................dollars on the...........day of..............;
and...................dollars at the expiration of the said........
months. And it is agreed that the said party of the second part shall be
at all the expense of manning, etc., and shall return the same to the
said party of the first part, at the port of...................., in as
good condition as it now is with exception of the ordinary use and
wear, and if the said party of the second part shall at any time refuse
to fulfill on his part, the said party of the first part shall have the right
to take possession of the said vessel, wherever the same be found.*

In Witness Whereof, *the said parties have hereunto set their hands
and seals, the day and year above written.*

Sealed and Delivered
  in presence of

................................(*Seal*)
................................(*Seal*)

**Chattel
Mortgage.**

See *Mortgage.*

Checks.

A check is an order in writing, without conditions, directing that the amount specified
be paid on demand to the order of the person or persons
named. A bill of exchange.

A person who draws a check on a bank in which he has
no account is guilty of a crime and liable to indictment.

A check should be presented at the bank for payment
as soon as possible after its receipt, usually within twenty-
four hours.

If the check is payable to the ORDER of some person named, the person so specified must endorse it.

The endorsement must be the same as the face of the check. If drawn to the order of "MARTHA WILLIAMS" it will not do to endorse the check "M. A. WILLIAMS."

When the payee signs only his name on the back of the check (called an endorsement in blank) it remains negotiable, transferable to others; but if the payee endorses it PAY TO JOHN SIMPSON, signing his name below, it becomes the property of John Simpson only. Had he endorsed it PAY TO THE ORDER OF JOHN SIMPSON (called an endorsement in full), and signed his name underneath, it would then be negotiable and transferable by John Simpson to another.

A check reading PAY TO BEARER or PAY TO CASH needs no endorsement. It is payable to anyone who presents it. If the check is cashed after having been lost or stolen, the maker of the check would be the loser. But when it is payable to the ORDER of Bearer or Cash, the payee, or one collecting the amount of the check from the bank, must endorse it.

If the name of the payee is misspelled on the face of the check, when endorsing it he should first write it as it appears on the face and underneath his name correctly written, i. e.,

EDWARD BROWN
EDOUARD BROWNE

If there is a difference in the amount specified in the "body" or written amount on the check and the numerals,

No. 1   NEW YORK, January 1st, 1916

Statetown Bank & Trust Company

PAY TO THE ORDER OF MARY SMITH – – – – – – –

Two hundred fifty and $\frac{00}{100}$ – – – – – – DOLLARS

$250.$\frac{00}{100}$ _Charles Brown_

A PROPERLY DRAWN CHECK.

Mary Smith

ENDORSEMENT ON BACK OF CHECK.

No. 2   NEW YORK, January 3d, 1916

Statetown Bank & Trust Company

PAY TO THE ORDER OF   Bearer

Fifteen – – – – – – – DOLLARS

$ 15.$\frac{00}{100}$ _B. R. Smith_

AN IMPROPERLY DRAWN CHECK.

the bank is governed by the written amount; for example, if the body of the check states Two Hundred Fifty and $\frac{No}{100}$ Dollars and the numerals read $215.$\frac{50}{100}$, the bank pays $250.

While it is not necessary it is clearer to insert AND between the dollars and cents in the body of the check.

In drawing a check to the order of a married woman, it may be drawn either to (Mrs.) John Smith or to Mary Smith, but the latter is the better form unless it is desired to show it is the wife of "John Smith." The essential point is to endorse the check EXACTLY as it is drawn on the face.

A glance at check No. 2 on page 47 will show how easily it might be raised. The "Fifteen" is written so far to the right that "One Hundred" might readily be put before it and the numeral "1" as easily inserted before the figure "15", the check then calling for "One Hundred Fifteen" dollars instead of "Fifteen."

The Congress of the United States had under consideration some years ago a law to prohibit corporations from transmitting checks for less than One Dollar. It never became effective. A check may be issued for any amount. If less than One Dollar, the amount should be spelled out, followed by the word *only*: i. e., "Sixty-five cents only."

ALTERATIONS—A bank will not pay a check on which there is any evidence of alteration, except that the name of the bank printed on the check may be crossed out and the name of another bank, in which the drawer of the check has funds, may be substituted.

VOUCHER CHECK OF

STATETOWN HARBOR TERMINAL RAILWAY
STATETOWN, NEW YORK

PAY TO.. 191

....

INVOICE DATE	ORDER NO.	DESCRIPTION	AMOUNT

Examined and Entered on Voucher Record   Certified as Correct   ?   Approved for Payment

By............................   By............................   By............................

BOOKKEEPER   **ENGINEER**   **PRESIDENT**

VOUCHER CHECK No.............................. $............................

RECEIVED FROM **STATETOWN HARBOR TERMINAL RAILWAY**

.... Dollars

Being in Full Payment of Above Account.

....PAYEE

When properly receipted this Voucher Check payable at

SMITH, JONES & CO.
TOWNSTATE, MD.

Statetown Harbor Terminal Railway

By............................

TREASURER

(Fold Voucher but once)

FORM OF VOUCHER CHECK.

VOUCHER CHECK No...............

Statetown Harbor Terminal Railway

PAYABLE TO   191

Month of $

DISTRIBUTION

FORM OF ENDORSEMENT OF VOUCHER CHECK.

Voucher Check—Check and receipt in one document, showing what payment by check covers. Usually drawn in duplicate.

Checks are numbered consecutively, the stub remaining in the check-book containing a corresponding number to the issued check. Some firms, when their cancelled checks are returned from the bank, have each check pasted to its stub.

Payment of Check Refused—See *Protest*.

Stop Payment Order—An order given by a customer to his bank directing it not to pay a specified check. When a check has been lost or stolen a "Stop Payment Order" should at once be sent to the bank.

January 1, 1916.

Statetown Bank & Trust Co.,
              Statetown,
                        New York.

Dear Sirs:

          Please accept this as notice that we desire payment stopped on our Check No. 333, dated December 28th, 1915, issued in favor of JOHN BROWN & COMPANY, for $250.

                    Yours truly,

                         (Sgd) MOORE & COMPANY

Form of Stop Payment Order.

CERTIFIED CHECK—When a bank "certifies" a check it guarantees that the drawer of the check has sufficient funds on deposit with it at the time to pay the check, and, except as to endorsements, the bank assumes liability for the payment. The amount of the check "certified" is immediately charged to the drawer's account.

EXCHANGE ON CHECKS—A collection charge on out-of-town checks, established by the Clearing House Associations.

SIGNATURE—When an account is opened, the depositor's signature is filed with the bank, and it is the duty of the bank to take every precaution against a forged or raised check being paid from the depositor's account. In some instances the bank is held liable, but not where the check has been carelessly drawn, as the example of "An improperly drawn check" hereinbefore shown.

OVERDRAW AN ACCOUNT—To draw against an account with a bank for an amount larger than stands to the credit of the drawer. This is a failing accredited by bankers to many women. It is related that one woman upon being notified by the bank that her account was overdrawn, promptly drew another check to cover the "overdraft."

ACTIVE ACCOUNT—One against which many checks are drawn and deposited.

DEPOSIT SLIP—A slip furnished by the bank to be filled out and turned in with each deposit, a check being made against the items on the printed slip to show what the deposit consists of, whether Bills and/or Specie (coins) and/or Checks.

See *Pass Book*.

DEPOSITED BY

SPENCER SMITH

—IN—

Statetown Bank

New York, Jan. 1st , *191*6

	Dollars	Cents
Bills (10's)	1 300	00
Specie (silver)	125	00
Checks		
" First State	100	00
" First Nat'l	350	00
" Corn Nat'l	200	00
	2 075	00

FORM OF DEPOSIT SLIP.

FOR DEPOSIT
Martha Williams
May 1, 1916

ENDORSEMENT ON CHECKS
FOR DEPOSIT.

FOR DEPOSIT ONLY IN
STATETOWN BANK
& TRUST CO.
for credit of
Martha Williams

FOR DEPOSIT TO THE
CREDIT OF
John Simpson

ENDORSEMENTS ON CHECKS FOR DEPOSIT.

Clearing House Association. An association of banks and trust companies through which daily exchange of notes and checks is made. Loans are also made to the various bank members of the association. There are about 200 clearing houses located throughout the United States. The Clearing House Association located in New York City was established in 1853.

Closed Mortgage. See *Mortgage.*

Codes. CIVIL—Statutes or system of laws determining the civil relations of citizens.

PENAL—Statutes defining crimes and regulating the method and degree of punishment.

Telegraphic—See *Cablegrams* and *Telegrams.*

Codicil. See *Wills.*

Coffee Exchange. Located on Pearl Street, New York City. Incorporated in 1885. Membership about 320. Provides a daily market where coffee may be bought and sold.

Collateral. Money or property deposited with a bank or individual at the time of obtaining a loan as security for the repayment of the amount borrowed. In case of default, such collateral security can be confiscated immediately, without having recourse to legal proceedings.

Coins.   Foreign value of:

Country	Standard.	Monetary Unit.	Value.
			D. C. M.
Argentine Republic.........	Gold.....	Peso.................	0 96 5
Austria-Hungary..........	Gold.....	Crown................	0 20 3
Belgium.................	Gold.....	Franc................	0 19 3
Bolivia.................	Gold.....	Boliviano............	0 38 9
Brazil..................	Gold.....	Milreis..............	0 54 6
Canada.................	Gold.....	Dollar...............	1 0 0
Costa Rica..............	Gold.....	Colon................	0 46 5
Chile..................	Gold.....	Peso.................	0 36 5
China..................	Silver....	Tael.... {Shanghai.... Haikwan..... (Customs)...	0 69 2 / 0 77 1
Colombia...............	Gold.....	Dollar...............	1 0 0
Denmark...............	Gold.....	Crown................	0 26 8
Ecuador...............	Gold.....	Sucre................	0 48 7
Egypt.................	Gold.....	Pound (100 piastres)...	4 94 3
Finland...............	Gold.....	Mark................	0 19 3
France.................	Gold.....	Franc................	0 19 3
German Empire..........	Gold.....	Mark................	0 23 8
Great Britain.............	Gold.....	Pound Sterling........	4 86 6½
Greece.................	Gold.....	Drachma..............	0 19 3
Hayti.................	Gold.....	Gourde...............	0 96 5
India (British)...........	Gold.....	Rupee...............	0 32 4⅓
Italy..................	Gold.....	Lira.................	0 19 3
Japan.................	Gold.....	Yen.................	0 49 8
Liberia................	Gold....	Dollar...............	1 0 0

Commissary. An official or department having charge of the food supply or the dispensing of other necessities.

Common Carrier. A person or corporation whose business it is to carry goods from one place to another for the public generally. Express companies, steamship and railroad companies, and others engaged in transportation generally, are COMMON CARRIERS.

Company. An association of two or more persons under a firm name for the purpose of conducting a business. A JOINT company enjoys some of the privileges of a corporation, the capital being divided into shares. A LIMITED company is one wherein the liability of the partners or shareholders is limited to the amount of capital they have put in or shares they own. See also *Corporation, By-laws, Bonds and Stocks.*

Compositor.   One who sets type.

Compound Interest.   See *Interest.*

Consignee.   The person to whom goods are directed.

Consignor.   The one who sends the goods to the receiver or consignee.

Consolidated Exchange.   Located corner Beaver and Broad Streets, New York City. Organized in 1886. Deals in odd lots, that is, in less than 100 shares. Securities listed upon the New York Stock Exchange are largely traded in, with some that are not listed on the Stock Exchange, such as mining stocks. While the rules of the Consolidated Exchange provide for the dealing in petroleum, grain and other products, wheat is the only one actively dealt in, and this in quantities less than permitted on the Produce Exchange (5,000 bushels). Seats on the Consolidated Exchange command about $2,000.

The New York Stock Exchange has a rule that any communication (with the Consolidated Exchange) by means of messenger, or clerks, or in any other manner, directly or indirectly between the New York Stock Exchange Building, or any part thereof, or any office of any member of said New York Stock Exchange or any part thereof, or any room, place, hallway or space occupied or controlled by said Consolidated Exchange, or any office of any member of said Consolidated Stock Exchange * * * through any means, apparatus, device or contrivance as above mentioned, is detrimental to the interest and welfare of this Exchange, and is hereby prohibited. That any member of this Exchange who transacts any business directly or indirectly with or for any member of said Consolidated Stock Exchange who is engaged in business upon said Consolidated Stock Exchange, shall, on conviction thereof, be deemed to have committed an act or acts detrimental to the interest and welfare of this Exchange.

Consols.   Contraction of "Consolidated Funds." (British.)

Contraband. Goods which a neutral is forbidden to furnish a belligerent country. Anything forbidden.

Contract.   A formal agreement between two or more parties, with a specified consideration, under which mutual rights or obligations are established. A contract may be either in writing or verbal. The "Acts of Providence or War" ever abrogate a contract. See *Agreement, Sunday Contracts* and *Business Laws*.

FORM OF BLANK CONTRACT.

Articles of Agreement, *Between...............................*

..of the first part,

and *...*

..of the second part,

The part......of the first part, in consideration of..............

covenant...and agree to ....

The part......of the second part, in consideration of..............

covenant....and agree to...

In Witness Whereof, *the parties hereunto have set their hands and*

seals the.............day of................in the year one thousand

nine hundred and............

Sealed and Delivered in the presence of

Conveyance.   A deed which passes or conveys land or property from one person to another.

Copy.   Manuscript which is to be set up in type.

Copyright.   Claim filed by an author or artist in the Copyright Office at Washington, D. C., of his exclusive right to publish or distribute his work for a period of twenty-eight years. To secure copyright registration under the Act of March 4, 1909, as amended, the following steps are necessary.

Ascertain to which of the following classifications the work belongs and write to the Register of Copyrights at Washington, D. C., for the form of application covering it, designating the number.

Class	Form No. of Application
(a) Books, including composite encyclopaedic works, directories, gazetteers, and other compilations. Reproduced in copies for sale.............	A 1
(b) Periodicals, newspapers. Single issue	B 1
(c) Lectures, sermons, addresses, prepared for oral delivery	C
(d) Dramatic or dramatico-musical compositions. Published dramatic composition for sale....	D 1
Dramatic compositions, copies not reproduced for sale	D 2
Published dramatico-musical composition...	D 3
(e) Musical compositions. Published for the first time................	E
Republished with new copyright............	E 1
Copies not reproduced for sale.............	E 2
(f) Maps	F
(g) Works of art; models or designs for works of art	G
(h) Reproductions of a work of art..............	H
(i) Drawings or plastic works of a scientific or technical character. Reproduced in copies for sale..............	I 1
Not reproduced in copies for sale...........	I 2
(j) Photographs. Reproduced in copies for sale..............	J 1
Not reproduced in copies for sale..........	J 2
(k) Prints and pictoral illustrations..............	K
(l) Motion-picture photoplays. Reproduced in copies for sale..............	L 1
Not reproduced in copies for sale...........	L 2
(m) Motion-pictures other than photoplays. Reproduced in copies for sale..............	M 1
Not reproduced in copies for sale...........	M 2

For Works Reproduced in Copies for Sale.

1.   Publish the work with copyright notice. The notice should read: "Copyright, 19.... (year date of publication) by............(name of copyright proprietor)." The date in the copyright notice should agree with the year date of publication.

2. Promptly after publication* send to the Copyright Office two copies of the best edition of the work, with an application for registration and a money order payable to the Register of Copyrights for the statutory registration fee of one dollar. As to special fee for registration of photographs, see *Works Not Reproduced in Copies for Sale.*

In the case of books the copies deposited must be accompanied by an affidavit, under the official seal of an officer authorized to administer oaths, stating that the typesetting, printing and binding of the book have been performed within the United States. Affidavit and application forms will be supplied by the Copyright Office upon request.

This affidavit is not required in the case of a book of foreign origin in a language or languages other than English, nor in the case of a printed play in any language, as such works are not required to be manufactured in the United States.

In the case of contributions to periodicals send one complete copy of the periodical containing the contribution with application and fee. No affidavit is required.

Only one copy is required to be deposited in the case of a work by an author who is a citizen or subject of a foreign state or nation and which has been published in a foreign country.

---

* Section 62 of the Copyright Law defines "the date of publication" as "the earliest date when copies of the first authorized edition were placed on sale, sold, or publicly distributed by the proprietor of the copyright or under his authority."

For Works Not Reproduced in Copies for Sale.

Copyright may also be had of certain classes of works (see a, b, c, etc., below) of which copies are not reproduced for sale, by filing in the Copyright Office an application for registration, with the statutory fee of one dollar, sending therewith:

(a)   In the case of lectures or other oral addresses, or of dramatic or musical compositions, one complete manuscript or typewritten copy of the work.

(b)   In the case of photographs not intended for general circulation, one photographic print. As to special fee see below.

(c)   In the case of works of art (paintings, drawing, sculpture) or of drawings or plastic works of a scientific or technical character, one photograph or other identifying reproduction of the work.

(d)   In the case of motion-picture photoplays, a title and description, with one print taken from each scene or act.

(e)   In the case of motion-pictures other than photoplays, a title and description, with not less than two prints taken from different sections of a complete motion-picture.

In the case of the works here noted, not reproduced in copies for sale, the law expressly requires that a second deposit of printed copies for registration and the payment of a second fee must be made upon publication.

The statutory fee for registration of any work, except a photograph, is one dollar, including a certificate of registration under seal. In the case of a photograph, if a certificate is not demanded the fee is fifty cents. In the case of several volumes of the same book deposited at the same time, only one registration at one fee is required.

Checks will not be accepted for payment of copyright fees. Remittances should be made by money order or bank draft.

Under the provisions of the "Act to Increase the Internal Revenue" approved October 22, 1914, a ten-cent documentary revenue stamp will be required to be attached to each certificate issued by the Copyright Office. The stamp should be forwarded at the time of application for registration of copyright, pinned to a card of the following form, which will be furnished upon request.

The ten-cent revenue stamp pinned to this card is to be used on the certificate of copyright to be issued to:

Write here the name of the claimant (OWNER) of copyright--

Write here the address to which certificate is to be sent----------------------------------

----

PIN HERE
10-cent revenue stamp or envelope containing necessary stamps

SEND TO REGISTER OF COPYRIGHTS, LIBRARY OF CONGRESS, WASHINGTON, D. C.

Office notation: Attached   to certificate Class---- No.--------

---

Following is the form of an Application and Affidavit furnished by the Copyright Office upon request:

Fill out each numbered space
APPLICATION FOR COPYRIGHT—BOOK   MANUFACTURED IN THE UNITED STATES

REGISTER OF COPYRIGHTS, Washington, D. C.   Date (1)_____

Of the BOOK named herein TWO complete copies of the best edition first published on the date stated herein are herewith deposited to secure copyright registration, accompanied by the AFFIDAVIT required by section 16 of the Act of March 4, 1909, that the book has been produced in accordance with the manufacturing provisions specified in section 15 of the said Act. $1 (statutory fee for registration and certificate) is also inclosed. The copyright is claimed by

Name and address of
  copyright claimant: (2)_____
      (Write name in full)

_____
      (Street)   (City)   (State)
Name of author, but if a
translation, then Translator (3)_____
      (Write name in full)

Country of which the author or translator is a citizen or subject (4)_____[Must be stated]
An alien author domiciled in the United
States must name the place of domicile (5)_____

Title of book (6)_____

_____ vol._____ Price $_____

- -

Leave all spaces within these double lines blank

	A1	$ a. rec'd_____
		Application rec'd
		Affidavit rec'd
		XX a._____
Fee rec'd $		

- -

Exact date of first
  publication (7)_____[State here the day, month, and year when the work was placed on sale, sold, or publicly distributed]

Send certificate of
  registration to (8)_____

_____
      (Street)   (City)   (State)
Name and address of person
  sending the fee: (9)_____

[Please turn this over]   (Street)   (City)   (State)

APPLICATION FOR COPYRIGHT-BOOK.

If a person wishes to deposit a sum of money to constitute a fund to be drawn on for successive registrations, he may do so.

A copyright may be assigned, and the assignment recorded within three months thereafter in the Copyright Office at Washington, D. C., for a fee of one dollar. After an assignment has been recorded in the Copyright Office the assignee may substitute his name for that of the

AFFIDAVIT (WHICH MUST BE MADE BY AN INDIVIDUAL, NOT A CORPORATION, AF-
TER PUBLICATION) OF AMERICAN MANUFACTURE OF COPYRIGHT BOOK.
Fill in the required statements to accord with the facts concerning the book named, and draw pen through
such statements as are not intended to be made.

State of_____
}
Notary's
Impression seal
here
County of_____
}ss.

I,_____

_____

_____, {being duly sworn, depose} and say:
{do solemnly affirm}

(1) That I am the person claiming copyright in the book named herein.
(2) That I am the duly authorized agent or representative residing in the United States
of the claimant of copyright in the book named herein.
(3) That I am the printer of the book named herein.
I further depose and say that, as required by the Act of March 4, 1909, the book entitled

_____

_____

of which two copies have been deposited, has been printed by_____
(Name of establishment)

_____ at _____
(City)   (State)
from {type}
{plates made in the U. S. from type} set within the limits of the United States by

_____
(Name of establishment)
that the printing of the text of
at_____; the said book was completed on_____, 19___;
(City)   (State)
that the said book was published on_____, 19___;
that the binding of the said book has been performed within the limits of the United States

by_____ at_____
(Name of establishment)   (City)   (State)

_____
(Signature of person making affidavit)

Subscribed and {sworn to}before me this_____day of_____, 19____.
{affirmed}
NOTICE.
If the date of publication is stated in the affidavit,
then the execution of this affidavit MUST BE SUB-   _____
SEQUENT to the publication of the book.   (Signature of Notary Public)
The notary is requested to see that this blank is
properly filled and that there are no variances or   _____
serious defects. PLEASE PLACE SEAL AT TOP.   [Oct., 1915]   [Please turn this over]

AFFIDAVIT ON BACK OF APPLICATION.

assignor in the statutory notice of copyright in the work
assigned, provided the transfer of proprietorship, as well
as the assignment of copyright, is recorded at Washington. An additional fee of ten cents is charged for this.

A copyright may be renewed within one year before the
expiration of the original twenty-eight year period for
another twenty-eight years.

EXTRACT FROM THE ACT OF MARCH 4, 1909, RE-
SPECTING THE COPYRIGHT NOTICE.

The notice of copyright required by Section Nine of this
Act shall consist of the word "Copyright" or the abbreviation "Copr.", accompanied by the name of the copyright proprietor, and if the work be a printed, literary, musical or
dramatic work, the notice shall include also the year in
which the copyright was secured by publication. In case,
however, of copies of works specified in sub-sections (f) to
(k)* inclusive of Section Five of this Act, the notice may
consist of the letter C inclosed within a circle, thus Ⓒ,
accompanied by the initials, monogram, mark or symbol of
the copyright proprietor: provided, that on some accessible
portion of such copies or of the margin, back, permanent
base or pedestal, or of the substance on which such copies
shall be mounted, his name shall appear. But in the case
of works in which copyright is subsisting when this Act shall
go into effect, the notice of copyright may be either in one
of the forms prescribed herein or in one of those prescribed
by the Act of June 18, 1874.

The notice of Copyright shall be applied in the case of a
book or other printed publication upon its title page or the
page immediately following (the back of the title page), or
if a periodical either upon the title page or upon the first
page of text of each separate number or under the title
heading, or if a musical work either upon its title page or the
first page of music; provided, that one notice of copyright
in each volume or in each number of a newspaper or periodical published shall suffice.

Corner.   A stock is said to be *cornered* when a certain clique get possession of the majority
shares of a particular company and by manipulation force
the prices above normal.

---

* The following are the classes of works "specified in sub-sections (f) to
   (k) :"
(f)   Maps ;
(g)   Works of art; models or designs for works of art;
(h)   Reproductions of a work of art ;
(i)   Drawings or plastic works of a scientific or technical character;
(j)   Photographs ;
(k)   Prints and pictorial illustrations.

Photograph by Logan and Bryan. From Underwood & Underwood, N. Y.

A SCENE IN THE "PIT" OF THE NEW YORK COTTON EXCHANGE

Corporation. A permanent organization, with the privilege in some states of perpetual succession*, endowed with the right to conduct business as an individual. See also *By-laws, Charter, Company* and *Stockholders.*

Cotton Exchange. Located in Hanover Square, New York. Incorporated in 1871. Membership limited to 450. Through it is financed and distributed about four-fifths of the cotton crop of this country. Traders from all parts of the world buy and sell on this exchange.

Coupon. One of a series of small certificates attached to a bond, representing the interest due quarterly, semi-annually or annually, at a fixed rate. When the interest is due, the coupon is cut from the bond and presented to the bank, banker, broker or trust company where payment is to be made, or it may be deposited in a bank the same as a check or cash.

NO. 1000   **$25.00**

Upon the first day of May, 1916, the CALCUTTA TIMBER COMPANY will pay to bearer at its office or agency in the City of New York, **Twenty-five Dollars,** *($25.00) gold coin of the United States of America, being six months interest then due on its first mortgage five per cent. gold bond No. 1000, unless said bond shall have been previously paid before maturity as provided therein.*

                        Treasurer.

FORM OF COUPON.

---

* In New York State, the following constitutional amendment to end the granting of perpetual franchise to public service corporations is before the Legislature: "Neither the Legislature, nor any municipality or corporation shall grant any franchise in perpetuity. Franchises for fixed or for indeterminate periods may be granted on conditions that shall permit the grantor to resume control thereof upon terms to be embodied in the original grant. Upon such resumption of control of any franchise, compensation shall not be granted for the franchise, but only for the actual cost, less depreciation, of the physical property devoted to the operation of such franchise."

Covenant. A modifying or qualifying agreement contained within another agreement or deed. A separate agreement in any instrument under seal.

Creditor. One to whom a debt is due.

Curb Market. The Hughes Commission, appointed to investigate the New York Stock Exchange, included in its report, dated June 7, 1909, the following with reference to the Curb Market:

> "There is an unorganized stock-market held in the open air during exchange hours. It occupies a section of Broad Street. An enclosure in the center of the roadway is made by means of a rope, within which the traders are supposed to confine themselves, leaving space on either side for the passage of street traffic; but during days of active trading the crowd often extends from curb to curb. There are about 200 subscribers, of whom probably 150 appear on the curb each day, and the machinery of the operations requires the presence of as many messenger boys and clerks. * * *
>
> This open-air market, we understand, is dependent for the great bulk of its business upon members of the Stock Exchange, approximately 85% of the orders executed on the curb coming from Stock Exchange houses. The Exchange itself keeps the curb market in the street, since it forbids its own members engaging in any transactions in any other security exchange in New York. If the curb were put under a roof and organized, this trading could not be maintained.
>
> The curb market has existed for upwards of thirty years, but only since the great development of trading in securities began, about the year 1897, has it become really important. It affords a public market place where all persons can buy and sell securities which are not listed on any organized exchange * * *."

Subsequently, in 1910, the New York Curb Market Association was formed with a membership of 250; annual dues $100.

Stocks of many of the large corporations whose securities are not listed on the New York Stock Exchange, such as the Standard Oil Co., are dealt in on the Curb, as well as stocks that have been issued but not yet listed on the Stock Exchange.

Customs and Duties. Customs (always plural)—Tariffs or duties levied on exports and imports. Under the United States Customs Laws and Regulations, a resident of the United States returning thereto is entitled to bring with him FREE OF DUTY personal effects taken abroad by him as baggage PROVIDED they have not been remodeled or improved abroad so as to increase their value, and in addition thereto articles of wearing apparel or adornments of the person, purchased or otherwise obtained abroad of a total value NOT EXCEEDING $100, provided they are properly declared, not for sale nor intended for other persons.

Days of Grace. The extra time (usually three days) allowed after a note or bill becomes due before payment is demanded.

Dead Freight. Money paid to the owners of a vessel for space that was booked for cargo but not filled.

Debenture. A bond or written acknowledgment of a debt. A promise to pay.

INTEREST LAWS AND STATUTES OF LIMITATION.

States and Territories	Interest Laws		Statutes of Limitations			States and Territories	Interest Laws		Statutes of Limitations		
	Legal Rate	Rate Allowed by Contract	Judgments Years	Notes Years	Open Accounts Years		Legal Rate	Rate Allowed by Contract	Judgments Years	Notes Years	Open Accounts Years
	Per cent.	Per cent.					Per cent.	Per cent.			
Alabama	8	8	20	6	3	Montana	8	Any rate	10(b)	8	5
Alaska	8	12	10	6	1	Nebraska	7	10	5‡‡	5	4
Arkansas	6	10	10	5	3	Nevada	7	Any rate	6	4	4
Arizona	6	Any rate	5	4	3	N. Hampshire	6	6	20	6	6
California	7	Any rate	5	4	4	New Jersey	6	6	20	6	6
Colorado	8	Any rate	20	6	6	New Mexico	6	12	7	6	4
Connecticut	6	Any rate	(o)	(e)	6	New York	6	6††	20(n)	6	6§§
Delaware	6	6	10	6‖	3	N. Carolina	6	6	10	3*	3
D. of Columbia	6	10	12	3	3	North Dakota	7	12	10(m)	6	6§§
Florida	8	10	20	5‖	2	Ohio	6	8	15(p)	15	6
Georgia	7	8	7	6‖	4	Oklahoma	6	10	5(h)	5	3
Hawaii	8	12	20(n)	6	6	Oregon	6	10	10	6	6
Idaho	7	12	6	5	4	Pennsylvania	6	6	5(f)	6‖	6
Illinois	5	7	20	10	5	Porto Rico	6	12	(q)	(q)	(q)
Indiana	6	8	20	10	6	Rhode Island	6§	Any rate	20	6	6
Iowa	6	8	20(d)	10	5	So. Carolina	7	8	10	6	6
Kansas	6	10	5	5	3	South Dakota	7	12	10(l)	6	6
Kentucky	6	6	15	15	5(a)	Tennessee	6	6	10	6	6
Louisiana	5	8	10	5	3	Texas	6	10	10‡‡	4	2
Maine	6	Any rate	20	6(c)	6§§	Utah	8	12	8	6	4
Maryland	6	6	12	3	3	Vermont	6	6	8	6	6§§
Massachusetts	6	Any rate	20	6	6	Virginia	6	6	20	5*	2¶
Michigan	5	7 ·	10	6	6	Washington	6	12	6	6	3
Minnesota	6	10	10	6	6	West Virginia	6	6	10	10	5
Mississippi	6	10	7	6	3	Wisconsin	6	10	20(n)	6	6
Missouri	6	8	10	10	5	Wyoming	8	12	21	5	8

* Under seal, 10 years. § Unless a different rate is expressly stipulated. ‖ Under seal, 20 years. ¶ Store accounts; other accounts 3 years; accounts between merchants 5 years. †† New York has by a recent law legalized any rate of interest on call loans of $5,000 or upward, on collateral security. ‡‡ Becomes dormant, but may be revived. §§ Six years from last item. (a) Accounts between merchants 2 years. (b) In courts not of record 5 years. (c) Witnessed 20 years. (d) Twenty years in Courts of Record; in Justice's Court 10 years. (e) Negotiable notes 6 years, non-negotiable 17 years. (f) Ceases to be a lien after that period, unless revived. (h) On foreign judgments 1 year. (l) Ten years foreign, 20 years domestic. (m) Subject to renewal. (n) Not of record 6 years. (o) No limit. (p) Foreign. Domestic 6 years. (q) Varies from 3 to 30 years.

Penalties for Usury differ in the various states. California, Colorado, Maine, Massachusetts (except on loans of less than $1,000), Montana and Nevada have no provisions on the subject. Loss of *principal and interest* is the penalty in Arkansas and New York. Loss of principal in Delaware and Oregon.

Loss of interest in Alabama, Alaska, Arizona, District of Columbia, Florida, Idaho, Illinois, Iowa, Louisiana, Michigan, Minnesota, Mississippi, Nebraska, New Jersey, North Carolina (double amount if paid), North Dakota (double amount if paid), Oklahoma, Porto Rico, South Carolina, South Dakota, Texas, Virginia, Washington (double amount if paid), Wisconsin, Hawaii, and Wyoming.

Loss of excess of interest in Connecticut, Georgia, Indiana, Kansas, Kentucky, Maryland, Missouri, New Hampshire (three times), New Mexico, Ohio, Pennsylvania, Tennessee, Vermont, and West Virginia. Loss of principal and interest in Rhode Island, also fine or imprisonment.

—*World Almanac.*

Debts.   Each state has interest laws or "statutes of limitation" within which stated time an action must be brought to collect debts and claims. After this limit has expired, the debts are said to be "outlawed."

A judgment is usually good for twenty years.

Contracts under seal are good for a longer period than those not under seal.

In the majority of states, promissory notes are outlawed in six years, but in some states when under seal they are good for twenty years.

Deed.   A written instrument or conveyance, under seal, transferring title to real property. The seller is called the "grantor" and the buyer the "grantee." Before the execution of a deed, a contract of sale is usually entered into and the purchaser has the title to the property "searched" (see *Abstract of Title*) to ascertain whether the seller has actual title to the land and that there are no mortgages, liens or encumbrances against it. A deed should contain the names of the purchaser and seller (grantee and grantor), the date the deed is executed and a consideration. Frequently "One Dollar" is given as the "consideration" when it is not desired that the actual amount paid shall be known. A deed made by an infant under twenty-one years of age or an insane person is not valid, nor is a deed obtained by fraud or force.

DEED WITH FULL COVENANTS (NEW YORK FORM)

*This Indenture, made the ....day of ....
in the year nineteen hundred and ....*

𝔅etween ....of the first part and ....of the second part.

𝔚itnessetb *that the said part....of the first part, in consideration of ....Dollars, lawful money of the United States, paid by the part....of the second part, do....hereby grant, and release unto the said part....of the second part....heirs and assigns forever,*

𝔄ll

(*here insert description of property*)

𝔗ogetber *with the appurtenances and all the estate and rights of the part....of the first part in and to said premises.*

𝔗o bave anb to bolb *the above granted premises unto the said part... of the second part.... heirs and assigns forever.*

𝔄nb *the said ....part.... of the first part do...covenant with the said part....of the second part as follows :*
First — That ....the part... of the first part...seized of the said premises in fee simple and ha... good right to convey the same.
Second — That the part....of the second part shall quietly enjoy the said premises.
Third — That the said premises are free from incumbrances.
Fourth — That...the part....of the first part will execute or procure any further necessary assurances of the title to said premises.
Fifth — That...the part......of the first part will forever warrant the title to said premises.

𝔦n witness wbereof *the said part....of the first part ha....hereunto set...............hand.. and seal...the day and year first above written.*

....
(*Signature of grantor*).

𝔦n presence of
(*Witnesses*)

WARRANTY DEED—The grantor in a Warranty Deed guarantees to the grantee that the title is absolutely free and clear, and should it prove otherwise the grantee can recover any loss from the grantor.

QUIT CLAIM DEED—Merely a transfer of the right, title and interest in a property without responsibility for defects in the title.

TRUST DEED—Conveyance of title in a property to some person or company to be held in trust for others. The duty of the Trustee is to see that the provisions of the trust deed are carried out.

After a deed has been properly executed, it should be recorded in the office of the proper official (County Clerk, Register of Deeds). See *Release* and *Release of Dower*.

Demurrage. The compensation or allowance made for the delay of a vessel by the freighter beyond the time agreed upon. Also refers to delay to freight trains.

Demurrer. A pleading in law denying that a real or valid cause of action exists.

Deponent. One who makes an affidavit.

Deposition. The written testimony of a witness, who is located in a city or town distant from the one in which the case is to be tried, sworn to before a Notary Public or other duly commissioned officer, and used at the trial which he is unable or unwilling to attend.

Deposit. See *Checks*.

Depreciation. (Railroad term.) Wear and tear of railroad equipment, buildings, machinery, etc. A diminished value.

Difference in STANDARD TIME (From a statement pre-
Time. pared by the United States Naval Observa-
tory, Washington, D. C.) The United
States adopted standard time in 1883, on the initiative of
the American Railway Association, according to which the
meridians of 75°, 90°, 105° and 120° west from Greenwich became the time meridians of EASTERN, CENTRAL,
MOUNTAIN and PACIFIC standard time respectively.

Theoretically, the divisions should be half way between
the above meridians, but for general convenience (and
from the necessities of operation) the railroads change
their time at the ends of railroad divisions, so that Eastern
standard time is used from the Atlantic Coast to an irregular line through Buffalo, Salamanca, Pittsburgh, Wheel-
ing, W. Va.; Holloway, O.; Huntington, W. Va.; Bristol,
Tenn.; Norton, Va.; Asheville, N. C.; Atlanta, Augusta,
Ga.; Columbia, S. C.; Central Junction, Ga. Some of
these cities use Eastern and some Central time, while the
railroads use one time in one direction and the other time
in the other direction.

The same applies to the cities on the dividing lines between the Central and Mountain Divisions, the line running through Bismarck, N. D.; South Dakota, Nebraska,
Colorado, Kansas, New Mexico and Texas to El Paso; also
to the cities on the dividing line between the Mountain and
Pacific division, the line running through Montana, Idaho,
Oregon, Utah, Nevada and Arizona.

Almost all countries throughout the world use standard
time based on the meridians 15° apart from Greenwich,
while some use standard time based on the longitude of
their national observatories.—(*World Almanac.*)

ALIGNMENT OF STATES IN STANDARD TIME SECTIONS ALONG THE BORDERS OF THE SECTIONS.

Eastern Time.
Pennsylvania.*
West Virginia.*
Virginia.
North Carolina.
South Carolina.

Central Time.
North Dakota (Eastern part).
South Dakota (Eastern part).
Nebraska (Eastern part).
Kansas.
Oklahoma.
Texas.
Michigan.*
Ohio.*
Kentucky.
Tennessee.
Georgia.
Florida*

Mountain Time.
North Dakota (Western part).
South Dakota (Western part).
Nebraska (Western part).
Colorado.
New Mexico.
Montana.
Idaho.
Utah.
Arizona.

Pacific Time.
Washington.
Oregon.
Nevada.
California.

STANDARD TIME USED IN THE PRINCIPAL CITIES OF THE UNITED STATES.

Eastern Time	Central Time	Central Time	Mountain Time
Augusta, Ga.	Atlanta, Ga.	Minneapolis, Minn.	Denver, Colo.
Baltimore, Md.	Chicago, Ill.	Mobile, Ala.	Laramie, Wyo.
Bangor, Me.	Cincinnati, O.	Nashville, Tenn.	Leadville, Colo.
Boston, Mass.	Columbus, O.	New Orleans, La.	Salt Lake City
Buffalo, N. Y.	Des Moines, Ia.	Omaha, Nebr.	Colorado Springs
Charleston, S. C.	Galveston, Tex.	Pensacola, Fla.	Helena, Mont.
Columbia, S. C.	Hannibal, Mo.	Port Huron, Mich.	
New London, Ct.	Houston, Tex.	Quincy, Ill.	
New York, N. Y.	Indianapolis, Ind.	St. Joseph, Mo.	
Norfolk, Va.	Jefferson City, Mo.	St. Louis, Mo.	Pacific Time
Oswego, N. Y.	Kansas City, Mo.	St. Paul, Minn.	
Philadelphia, Pa.	Knoxville, Tenn.	San Antonio, Tex.	Kalama, Wash.
Pittsburgh, Pa.	Louisville, Ky.	Savannah, Ga.	Portland, Ore.
Portland, Me.	Lincoln, Nebr.	Selma, Ala.	San Francisco,
Providence, R. I.	Little Rock, Ark.	Sioux City, Ia.	Tacoma, Wash.
Richmond, Va.	Macon, Ga.	Vincennes, Ind.	Seattle, Wash.
Washington, D. C.	Memphis, Tenn.	Vicksburg, Miss.	
Wilmington, N. C.	Milwaukee, Wis.	Winona, Minn.	

* Established by State law. In other cases the use of uniform Standard Time is prescribed by decisions of the courts.

The time in other States more distant from the borders is obvious from the section in which they are located.

The times in use at points in the vicinity of the borders between Standard Time Sections, such as Buffalo, Pittsburgh, etc., are governed by the contingencies of operation of the several roads.

One hour's difference in time is reckoned between each division. When it is noon "Eastern Standard Time," it is 11 a. m. "Central Standard Time," 10 a. m. "Mountain Standard Time," and 9 a. m. "Pacific Standard Time."

DIFFERENCE IN STANDARD TIME BETWEEN PRINCIPAL CITIES.

CITIES	WHEN IT IS 12 O'CLOCK NOON ACCORDING TO			
	Eastern Time	Central Time	Mountain Time	Pacific Time
	IN THE UNITED STATES			
At	It is	It is	It is	It is
Aden....................Arabia	8.00 P.M.	9.00 P.M.	10.00 P.M.	12.00 M.
Amsterdam..............Holland	5.20 P.M.	6.20 P.M.	7.20 P.M.	8.20 P.M.
Athens...................Greece	6.35 P.M.	7.35 P.M.	8.35 P.M.	9.35 P.M.
Berlin..................Germany	6.00 P.M.	7.00 P.M.	8.00 P.M.	9.00 P.M.
Bombay...................India	9.51 P.M.	10.51 P.M.	11.51 P.M.	12.51 A.M.
Bremen.................Germany	6.00 P.M.	7.00 P.M.	8.00 P.M.	9.00 P.M.
Central Time........United States	11.00 A.M.	12.00 M.	1.00 P.M.	2.00 P.M.
Constantinople...........Turkey	6.56 P.M.	7.56 P.M.	8.56 P.M.	9.56 P.M.
Copenhagen.............Denmark	6.00 P.M.	7.00 P.M.	8.00 P.M.	9.00 P.M.
Dublin..................Ireland	4.35 P.M.	5.35 P.M.	6.35 P.M.	7.35 P.M.
Eastern Time.......United States	12.00 M.	1.00 P.M.	2.00 P.M.	3.00 P.M.
Hamburg...............Germany	6.00 P.M.	7.00 P.M.	8.00 P.M.	9.00 P.M.
Havre...................France	5.00 P.M.	6.00 P.M.	7.00 P.M.	8.00 P.M.
Hong Kong...............China	12.37 A.M.*	1.37 A.M.*	2.37 A.M.*	3.37 A.M.*
Honolulu................Hawaii	6.29 A.M.	7.29 A.M.	8.29 A.M.	9.29 A.M.
Liverpool..............England	5.00 P.M.	6.00 P.M.	7.00 P.M.	8.00 P.M.
London.................England	5.00 P.M.	6.00 P.M.	7.00 P.M.	8.00 P.M.
Madrid...................Spain	5.00 P.M.	6.00 P.M.	7.00 P.M.	8.00 P.M.
Manila........Philippine Islands	1.00 A.M.*	2.00 A.M.*	3.00 A.M.*	4.00 A.M.*
Melbourne............Australia	3.00 A.M.*	4.00 A.M.*	5.00 A.M.*	6.00 A.M.*
Mountain Time......United States	10.00 A.M.	11.00 A.M.	12.00 M.	1.00 P.M.
Pacific Time........United States	9.00 A.M.	10.00 A.M.	11.00 A.M.	12.00 M.
Paris....................France	5.00 P.M.	6.00 P.M.	7.00 P.M.	8.00 P.M.
Rome.....................Italy	6.00 P.M.	7.00 P.M.	8.00 P.M.	9.00 P.M.
Stockholm..............Sweden	6.00 P.M.	7.00 P.M.	8.00 P.M.	9.00 P.M.
St. Petersburg...........Russia	7.01 P.M.	8.01 P.M.	9.01 P.M.	10.01 P.M.
Vienna..................Austria	6.00 P.M.	7.00 P.M.	8.00 P.M.	9.00 P.M.
Yokohama................Japan	2.00 A.M.*	3.00 A.M.*	4.00 A.M.*	5.00 A.M.*

* Following day.

Great Britain adopted standard time in 1880; Sweden in 1879; Japan in 1886; Germany in 1892; Austria in 1891; Prussia in 1893; Italy in 1893; Switzerland in 1894; Denmark in 1894; Norway in 1895; Spain in 1901; and France in 1911.

Differential. The difference or dissimilarity between two things. (Railroad) The difference between the rates of two competing railroads to the same point.

Discount. The interest subtracted in advance from the amount stated on the face of a note or bill of exchange. A rebate on a bill in consideration of prompt or cash payment. The price of stocks or bonds below their par value; a stock or bond originally issued at $100 and sold at, say $98, is said to be sold at a DISCOUNT.

Disfranchise. To deprive of or take away a privilege, right, or grant. See *Franchise.*

Dividend. The percentage of profit that is distributed among the stockholders whose names appear on the books of the company. Profit on shares of stock. Stocks bought after the books of a company have been closed, are said to be bought "ex-dividend"—without dividend. When a company stops paying a dividend, it is said to "pass its dividend." See *Bonds and Stocks.*

Dower. See *Release of Dower* and *Wills.*

Draft. A written order from one party to another directing the payment of the amount named on its face within a specified time.

$_____$ NEW YORK,_____19___

AT SIGHT, PAY TO THE ORDER OF _____

_____ DOLLARS

VALUE RECEIVED, AND CHARGE THE SAME TO_____

ACCOUNT.

_____

FORM OF SIGHT DRAFT.

$_____$ NEW YORK,_____19___

THIRTY DAYS AFTER DATE, PAY TO THE ORDER

OF_____

_____ DOLLARS

VALUE RECEIVED, AND CHARGE TO_____ACCOUNT.

_____

FORM OF TIME DRAFT.

Draft with Stock Attached. The seller of the stock forwards the stock, with a draft upon the purchaser attached, to a bank, who presents the draft for collection, and upon payment delivers the stock to the purchaser.

Dress. The earnest business woman courting Success has enough business acumen to realize that personal appearance goes a long way toward conveying her "personality" to those with whom she must perforce come in contact. A plain, modestly dressed woman carries an air of self-respect and efficiency that will prove one of her chief assets in the business world.

In order to present a well-groomed, pleasing ensemble, no single part of her toilette predominates.

Good taste, breeding, discernment, intelligence, all demand that she shall dress *appropriately*. Just as certain clothes are proper for wear at the theater, the opera, formal dinners, afternoon tea, etc., so certain clothes are properly worn in the business office.

Accordion-pleated skirts; chiffon, satin, lace or fancy silk waists; large "picture" hats, or hats with plumes; brocaded or velvet suits: are frivolous fineries that have their place, but that place is not a business office.

It is true some firms considerately serve afternoon tea, but they do not expect their woman employees to dress for it!

Unblacked shoes, with run-down or French heels; unclean or highly-polished nails; a soiled or "peek-a-boo" shirtwaist; a badly hanging skirt, with underskirt showing; a suit that is over-trimmed or extreme in style; disheveled hair; a face powdered or rouged: are abominations either in or outside of a business office.

On the other hand, a becoming suit, dark in color and untrimmed; black shoes with common-sense or moderately high Cuban heels, polished daily; well-cared-for hands; a tailored, immaculately clean shirtwaist; a trim, well-cut skirt; hair simply and becomingly arranged, evidencing the proverbial "fifty-brushes-a-day" treatment; a small but smartly trimmed hat; an avoidance of extremes in style, or in fact anything in manners or clothes that would tend to make her conspicuous: are marks that identify the "lady" (using that term advisedly) in business.

To their credit be it said, very few business women offend against good taste by wearing excess of jewelry. A well chosen pin or lavalliere at the throat, one or perhaps two rings (showy diamonds are extremely vulgar in an office) and a watch, are the modest adornments permitted to the business woman.

Due Bill.   An instrument acknowledging in writing that a debt is owed.

$100

DUE HERBERT SMITH, OR BEARER, ONE HUNDRED DOLLARS IN MERCHANDISE, FOR VALUE RECEIVED, PAYABLE ON DEMAND.

FRANK ARBUCKLE.

NEW YORK, MARCH 1, 1916.

FORM OF DUE BILL PAYABLE IN GOODS.

Dun.   Publisher of commercial ratings.

Easement.   A right or convenience over the land of another, as a right of way, or water course.

Equipment.   All the rolling stock—locomotives, cars, etc. —of a railroad.   An outfit.

Equity.   The ownership in a property over and above

Escrow. Something deposited with a third party to be held in trust until certain acts have been performed, conditions fulfilled, or certain events have happened.

Et Al. And others.

Et Ux. And wife.

Exchange, Foreign. See *Coins, foreign value of.*

Executor. See *Wills.*

Ex Officio. By virtue of office.

F.O.B. Free on Board.

Face. The flat amount. The value exclusive of any deductions such as interest, discount, premium. The principal. See *Par.*

Fee Simple. That estate or interest which an owner holds to himself and his heirs forever. Absolute ownership, free and clear.

Feme Covert. A married woman.

Feme Sole. An unmarried woman.

Fiduciary. Trustee. Fiduciary Capacity, financial relation of trust, as between a guardian and ward, an executor and beneficiary of a will, an attorney and his client, a trustee and the recipient of trust funds, etc., etc.

Filing Systems. "To find that letter in the right place you must file it right in the first place," is the admonition of one of the large makers of filing systems.

The use of the letter-book with letter copying press has almost entirely given away to the carbon copy and the Rapid Roller Copier copy; both reproductions of correspondence being cared for in some one of the several vertical filing methods which have, for general correspondence, almost wholly superceded the old and various forms of flat filing.

Alphabetical Filing.

This is the most widely used, being the best adapted to average business requirements, consisting of a simple alphabetical arrangement of guides and folders reading from A to Z.

With such a system, you simply file in the "A" folder all papers that would naturally be indexed under "A"; all "B" papers in the "B" folder, etc. When there is considerable volume of correspondence with one firm or person, a special folder is made out and filed in front of the alphabetical folder. There may be several of these special folders behind each guide. All papers in each folder should be filed chronologically, that is, according to date, with the latest date in front.

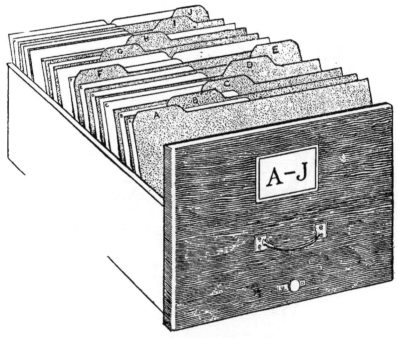

THE SIMPLEST ALPHABETICAL SYSTEM—ONE GUIDE FOR EACH LETTER OF ALPHABET.

(*Courtesy of Yawman & Erbe Mfg. Co.*)

NUMERICAL FILING.

For some uses, especially where a cross index to a file is necessary, no other method will serve so well as numerical indexing. Railroads, insurance companies, large corporations, etc., find it indispensable.

Take for example the subject file of a railroad company. Each subject is assigned to a number. All papers relating to that subject are numbered accordingly and filed behind numerical guides. For instance, take the subject of "Ac-

cidents" which is allotted to the number "18." Behind
the "18" guide is a folder for each accident on record.
These folders are numbered "18-1," "18-2", "18-3" etc.

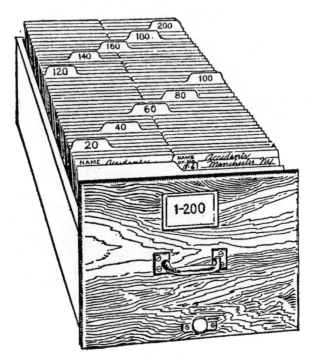

THE NUMERICAL SYSTEM.
(Courtesy of Yawman & Erbe Mfg. Co.)

Papers may be cross-indexed, for the matter sometimes
is referred to as an "accident" or "collision" or "wreck."
The card index will bear the number "18" and the word
"Accidents" at the top.

Every paper on the subject bears the file number. In
correspondence, the matter is referred to by number. Some
firms have printed on their letterheads "REFER TO FILE
........" or "WHEN REPLYING REFER TO FILE........"
This minimizes the chance of error or confusion.

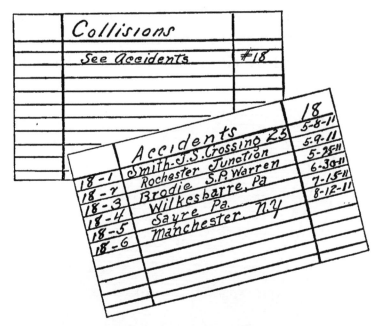

CROSS INDEX TO THE SUBJECT FILE OF A RAILROAD.

SUBJECT FILING.

For the stock-keeper or purchasing agent, the subject filing is found especially satisfactory. The file is first classed by "Articles," using a set of guides with tabs in three positions across the file. The guides are usually arranged alphabetically, the names of the various articles being plainly printed on the guide tabs. In railroad and steamship offices, where correspondence is heavy, Subject Filing in conjunction with Numerical Filing is used, together with a detailed card index.

GEOGRAPHICAL (OR LOCATION) FILING.

Divides the correspondence according to geographical divisions. It may be classified by states and divided with "state" guides arranged alphabetically or by sections. If the size of the correspondence warrants, a set of alphabetical guides indexed by cities may be placed behind each state guide.

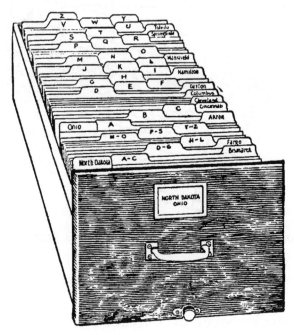

THE LATEST AND BEST GEOGRAPHICAL SYSTEM.
(*Courtesy of Yawman & Erbe Mfg. Co.*)

Correspondence should never be removed from the file unless a record is kept to tell WHERE it is. A colored sheet of paper is sometimes put in the place of the letter or document removed from the file and on it a memorandum is made of the date and other descriptive data, which quickly indicates the temporary absence of a letter or paper from the file.

Some one person should have entire charge of the filing and be held responsible for its proper operation.

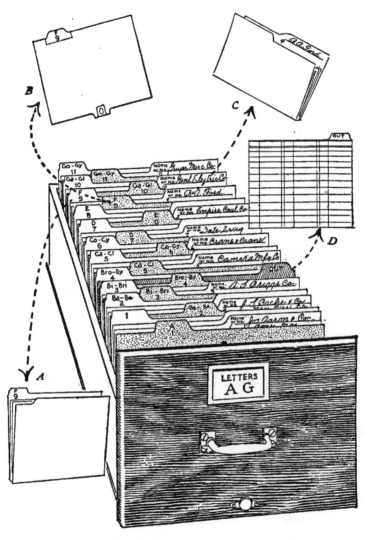

THE DIRECT NAME SYSTEM OF FILING, IN DETAIL.

(Courtesy of Yawman & Erbe Mfg. Co.)

A. The Alphabetical Numerical Folder for miscellaneous correspondence. Tabs act as guides in transfer file.

B. The Direct Name Guide. Odd numbers are in the left row, even numbers in the right—an additional aid in quick filing.

C. The Direct Name Folders for special correspondence are in a straight row, each its own guide. Folders are numbered, a check against mis-filing.

D. The "Out" Guide (usually colored) shows by whom correspondence has been removed. This is an efficient insurance against lost papers.

Finance.   Monetary transactions.

To raise or provide the necessary funds to carry out a commercial or public undertaking.

Fire Insurance.   Covers insurance on buildings and their contents. The premium or cost of the insurance varies with the value of the property, the location of it, the destructability of the contents, etc. A warehouse containing cotton commands a higher rate of insurance than an isolated building containing sheet iron, for instance.

Firm.   A company, partnership, association or business.

Fiscal Year.   A financial year, which, unlike a calendar year, may date from any month in the year.   At the close of a fiscal year, the books of a company are balanced to ascertain its financial condition.

Fixed Charges.   Permanent obligations that have to be met regularly, as interest, rent, taxes, insurance, etc.

Flat.   Without interest or modification.   Face value.

Floating Debt.   Obligations that are not permanent or fixed charges.

Fluctuation.   Changing.   The rising and falling of prices.

Foreclosure. A judicial proceeding taken by a mortgagee to recover payment for the money loaned, when the mortgagor has defaulted on the principal or interest of the mortgage. See *Mortgage.*

Franchise. A right, privilege or grant; as the RIGHT conferred on a corporation to conduct its business; the PRIVILEGE of voting; the GRANT of suffrage. Permission. A land patent granted by the Government in aid of railroad construction.

Funded Debt. Bonded indebtedness. Money loaned to a government or corporation.

Futures. The selling of something for future delivery. Sales made at prices based on speculation as to future condition of supply and demand.

Gilt-edged. Securities which are considered to be absolutely safe and upon which the interest is paid regularly and promptly when due. First class.

Gold Brick. Swindle.

Good Will. The value placed upon the friendly patronage of a business.

Government Bonds. Interest bearing obligations of a country. Bonds payable in gold of the present standard of weight and fineness. See *Standard of Weight and Fineness.*

Guarantee.
Guaranty. An assurance of payment. A promise or agreement to be responsible for the payment of a debt or the performance of some act or duty on the part of another.

```
┌──────────────────────────────────────────────┐
│                                                │
│  FOR VALUE RECEIVED..........................  │
│  GUARANTEES AND ASSURES THE PAYMENT OF THE     │
│  PRINCIPAL AND INTEREST OF THE FOREGOING MORT- │
│  GAGE AS AND WHEN SAME RESPECTIVELY COME DUE.  │
│                                                │
│  ............................................  │
│                                                │
└──────────────────────────────────────────────┘
```

FORM OF GUARANTY.

Habeas
Corpus. (Literally, "Produce the body"). An order directing that the body of one held in custody be produced in court. The Constitution of the United States provides: "the privilege of the writ of habeas corpus shall not be suspended, unless when in cases of rebellion or invasion the public safety may require it."

Hazard. Risk. See *Insurance.*

Heredita- Things which may be inherited.
ments.

Hypothecate. To deposit and pledge certain property as collateral security for a loan, which property is sold, in case of default, and the debt paid from the money realized. To pawn. See *Collateral.*

Ignorance of the Law. Ignorance of the law excuses no one. Everyone is bound to know the law and will not be excused from punishment by pleading ignorance of it.

Income Tax. See *Taxes*.

Indemnity. A guaranty to protect another against loss, damage or responsibility. See *Surety*.

Indenture. A legal instrument under seal; e.g., an Indenture of Mortgage, Lease, etc.

Indictment. A formal accusation against a person handed down by a grand jury charging a crime or misdemeanor.

Industrials. Stocks and bonds of a manufacturing company or corporation.

Infringement. The infraction or invasion of the rights of others, secured by copyright, patent or trade-mark.

Injunction. A prohibitory writ.

In Re. In the matter of.

Insolvent. Bankrupt. Unable to pay debts. Insufficient funds. See *Bankruptcy*.

In Statu Quo. As it was. In the same position.

Insurance. Indemnity against loss. See *Accident or Casualty, Life, Fire, Marine Insurance.* Policies of insurance are issued against loss of health, loss by burglary, lightning, covering workmen's compensation, employer's liability, fidelity insurance, etc.

A "rider" is a special schedule attached to a policy.

Interest. The rate or charge made for the employment of money. It is generally calculated on a percentage basis, a certain rate per annum. The money loaned is called the "principal"; the sum per cent. (per hundred) agreed upon for the use of the money is the rate of interest. Income.

SIMPLE INTEREST TABLE.

(Showing at Different Rates the Interest on $1 from 1 Month to 1 Year, and on $100 from 1 Day to 1 Year.)

Time.	4 Per Cent			5 Per Cent			6 Per Cent			7 Per Cent			8 Per Cent		
	Dollars.	Cents.	Mills.	Dollars.	Cents.	Mills.	Dollars.	Cents.	Mills.	Dollars.	Cents.	Mills.	Dollars.	Cents.	Mills.
One Dollar 1 month............			3			4			5			5			6
" " 2 months			7			8		1			1	1		1	3
" " 3 "		1	1		1	3		1	5		1	7		2	
" " 6 "		2			2	5		3			3	5		4	
" " 12 "		4			5			6			7			8	
One Hundred Dollars 1 day....		1	1		1	3		1	6		1	9		2	2
" " " 2 days		2	2		2	7		3	2		3	8		4	4
" " " 3 "		3	4		4	1		5			5	8		6	7
" " " 4 "		4	5		5	3		6	6		7	7		8	9
" " " 5 "		5	6		6	9		8	2		9	7		11	1
" " " 6 "		6	7		8	3		10			11	6		13	3
" " " 1 month .		33	4		41	6		50			58	3		66	7
" " " 2 months.		66	7		83	2	1			1	16	6	1	33	3
" " " 3 "	1			1	25		1	50		1	75		2		
" " " 6 "	2			2	50		3			3	50		4		
" " " 12 "	4			5			6			7			8		

World Almanac.

COMPOUND INTEREST TABLE.

COMPOUND INTEREST ON ONE DOLLAR FOR 100 YEARS.

Amount	Years	Per cent.	Accumulation	Amount	Years	Per cent.	Accumulation	Amount	Years	Per cent.	Accumulation
$1	100	1	$2.70,5	$1	100	4½	$81.58,9	$1	100	10	$13,780.66
1	100	2	7.24,5	1	100	5	131.50,1	1	100	11	34,064 34,6
1	100	2½	11.81,4	1	100	6	339.30,5	1	100	12	83,521.82,7
1	100	3	19.21,8	1	100	7	867.72,1	1	100	15	1,174,302.40
1	100	3½	31.19,1	1	100	8	2,199.78,4	1	100	18	15,424,106.40
1	100	4	50.50,4	1	100	9	5,529.04,4	1	100	24	2,198,720,200

YEARS IN WHICH A GIVEN AMOUNT WILL DOUBLE AT SEVERAL RATES OF INTEREST.

RATE	At Simple Interest	AT COMPOUND INTEREST			RATE	At Simple Interest	AT COMPOUND INTEREST		
		Compounded Yearly	Compounded Semi-Annually	Compounded Quarterly			Compounded Yearly	Compounded Semi-Annually	Compounded Quarterly
1	100 years	69.660	69.487	69.237	6	16.67	11.896	11.725	11.639
1½	66.66	46.556	46 382	46.297	6½	15.38	11.007	10.836	10.750
2	50.00	35.003	34.830	34.743	7	14.29	10.245	10.074	9 966
2½	40.00	28.071	27.899	27.748	7½	13.33	9.584	9.414	9.328
3	33 33	23.450	23 278	23.191	8	12 50	9.006	8.837	8.751
3½	28.57	20.149	19 977	19 890	8½	11.76	8.497	8.327	8 241
4	25.00	17.673	17.501	17.415	9	11.11	8.043	7.874	7.788
4½	22.22	15.747	15.576	15.490	9½	10 52	7.638	7.468	7.383
5	20.00	14.2C7	14.035	13.949	10	10.00	7.273	7.103	7.018
5½	18.18	12.942	12.775	12.689	12	8.34	6.116	5.948	5.862

World Almanac.

INTEREST CALCULATIONS.

RULE.—Multiply the principal by as many one hundredths as there are days, and then divide as follows:

Per cent,	4	5	6	7	8	9	10	12
Divide by	90	72	60	52	45	40	36	30

EXAMPLES.—Interest on $100. for 90 days at 5 per cent.: 100 x .90=9.00 divided by 72=1.25 (one dollar and 25 cents); on $1. for 30 days at 6 per cent.: 1 x .30=.300, divided by 60=.005 (5 mills).

TABLE.—Showing the number of days from any date in one month to the same date in any other month.

From To	Jan.	Feb.	Mch	April	May	June	July	Aug.	Sept.	Oct.	Nov	Dec.
January........	365	31	59	90	120	151	181	212	243	273	304	334
February.......	334	365	28	59	89	120	150	181	221	242	273	303
March..........	306	337	365	31	61	92	122	153	184	214	245	275
April..........	275	306	334	365	30	61	91	122	153	183	214	244
May............	245	276	304	335	365	31	61	92	123	153	184	214
June...........	214	245	274	304	334	365	30	61	92	122	153	133
July...........	184	215	243	273	304	335	365	31	62	92	123	153
August.........	153	184	212	243	273	304	334	365	31	61	92	122
September......	122	153	181	212	242	273	303	334	365	30	61	91
October........	92	123	151	182	212	243	273	304	335	365	31	61
November.......	61	92	120	151	181	212	242	273	304	334	365	30
December.......	31	62	90	121	151	182	212	243	274	304	335	365

EXAMPLE.—How many days from May 5th to October 5th? Look for May at left hand and October at the top; in the angle is 153. In leap-year add one day if February is included.

LEGAL RATE—Each state prescribes a fixed or "legal rate," higher than which is considered "usury," viz—

STATES AND TERRITORIES	DAYS OF GRACE.		INTEREST RATES.		STATUTES OF LIMITATIONS.		
	Notes.	Sight Drafts.	Legal.	Special or Contract.	Judgments, Years.	Notes, Years.	Open Accounts Years.
Alabama	No	No	8	8 per ct.	20	6*	3
Alaska	Yes	No	8	12 per ct.	10	6	1
Arizona	No	No	6	12 per ct.	5	4	3
Arkansas	Yes	Yes	6	10 per ct.	10	5	3
California	No	No	7	No limit.	5	4	4
Colorado	No	No	8	No limit.	20	6	6
Connecticut	No	No	6	No limit.	(a)	(b)	6
Delaware	No	No	6	6 per ct.	10	6†	3
District of Columbia	No	No	6	6 per ct.	12	3	3
Florida	No	No	8	10 per ct.	20	5	2
Georgia	Yes	No	7	8 per ct.	7	6†	4
Hawaiian Islands	No	No	8	12 per ct.	..	..	..
Idaho	No	No	7	12 per ct.	6	5	4
Illinois	No	No	5	7 per ct.	20	10	5
Indiana	No	No	6	8 per ct.	20	10	6
Iowa	No	No	6	8 per ct.	20‡	10	5
Kansas	No	No	6	10 per ct.	5	5	3
Kentucky	No	No	6	6 per ct.	15	15	5§
Louisiana	No	No	5	8 per ct.	10	5	3
Maine	No	Yes	6	No limit.	20	6–20	6
Maryland	No	No	6	6 per ct.	12	3	3
Massachusetts	No	Yes	6	No limit.	20	6	6
Michigan	No	No	5	7 per ct.	10	6	6
Minnesota	No	Yes	6	10 per ct.	10	6	6
Mississippi	Yes	Yes	6	10 per ct.	7	6	3
Missouri	No	No	6	8 per ct.	10	10	5
Montana	No	No	8	No limit.	10	8	5
Nebraska	No	No	7	10 per ct.	5	5	4
Nevada	Yes	No	7	No limit.	6	4	4
New Hampshire	No	Yes	6	6 per ct.	20	6	6
New Jersey	No	No	6	6 per ct.	20	6	6
New Mexico	Yes	Yes	6	12 per ct.	7	6	4
New York	No	No	6	‖ 6 per ct.	20	6	6
North Carolina	No	No	6	6 per ct.	10	3*	3
North Dakota	No	No	7	12 per ct.	10	6	6
Ohio	No	No	6	8 per ct.	6–15	15	6
Oklahoma	Yes	Yes	6	10 per ct.	1–5	5	3
Oregon	No	No	6	10 per ct.	10	6	6
Pennsylvania	No	No	6	6 per ct.	5	6†	6
Philippine Islands	No	No	6	No limit.	..	..	..
Porto Rico	No	No	6	12 per ct.	..	..	..
Rhode Island	No	Yes	6	No limit.	20	6	6
South Carolina	No	Yes	7	8 per ct.	10	6	6
South Dakota	Yes	Yes	7	12 per ct.	10	6	6
Tennessee	No	No	6	6 per ct.	10	6	6
Texas	Yes	Yes	6	6 per ct.	10	4	2
Utah	No	No	8	12 per ct.	8	6	4
Vermont	No	No	6	6 per ct.	8	6	6
Virginia	No	No	6	6 per ct.	20	5*	2–3
Washington	No	No	6	12 per ct.	6	6	3
West Virginia	No	No	6	6 per ct.	10	10	5
Wisconsin	No	No	6	10 per ct.	6–20	6	6
Wyoming	No	No	8	12 per ct.	21	5	8

‖ Any rate of interest on call loans of $5,000 or upward, on collateral security. (a) No limit. (b) Negotiable notes, 6 years. * Under seal, 10 years. † Under seal 20 years. ‡ In Courts of Record, 20 years; Justice's Court, 10 years. § Accounts between merchants 2

Interim Certificate. A temporary certificate used until the permanent certificates, which are engraved, lithographed or printed, have been issued.

Interstate Commerce Commission. The Interstate Commerce Commission was created by the act to regulate commerce, approved Feb. 4, 1887. The original act provided for five members at a salary of $7,500. Under the "Hepburn Act" approved June 29, 1906, the membership was increased to seven at a salary of $10,000 per annum and the term of office increased from six to seven years. Enlargement of the Commission is by appointment of the President by and with the advice and consent of the Senate.

The regulating statutes apply to all common carriers engaged in the transportation of oil or other commodity except water and except natural or artificial gas, by means of pipe lines, or partly by pipe line and partly by water, and to common carriers engaged in the interstate transportation of passengers or property wholly by railroad or partly by railroad and partly by water when both are used under a common control or management or a continuous carriage or shipment. Only traffic transported wholly within a single State is excepted. The commission has jurisdiction, on complaint, and after full hearing to determine and prescribe reasonable rates, regulations and practices and order reparation to injured shippers; to require any carriers to desist from unjust discrimination. Carriers must file annual reports with the Commission. Various other powers are conferred on the Commission.

Intestate. Having left no will; in which event an administrator of the decedent's estate is appointed by the court. See *Administrator.*

Inventory. An itemized list or schedule of property. A stock list.

Investment. Funds employed in such a manner as to secure a profitable and permanent income. The placing of funds in what is considered a safe enterprise, with the promise of moderate returns, as opposed to speculation. See *Building and Loan Associations, Bonds and Stocks, Municipals, Public Utilities, Government Bonds, Railroad Securities, Industrials, Savings Banks.*

LEGAL INVESTMENT—Stocks or Bonds in which the law of the state permits a savings bank to invest the funds of its depositors.

INCOME ON INVESTMENTS.
PAR VALUE $100.

Cost	4 per ct.	5 per ct.	6 per ct.	7 per ct.	8 per ct.	10 per ct.
$50.00	$8.00	$10.00	$12.00	$14.00	$16.00	$20.00
60.00	6.67	8.33	10.00	11.66	13.33	16.66
70.00	5.71	7.14	8.57	10.00	11.42	14.23
75.00	5.34	6.66	8.00	9.33	10.66	13.35
80.00	5.00	6.25	7.50	8.75	10.00	12.50
85.00	4.70	5.88	7.05	8.23	9.41	11.76
90.00	4.44	5.55	6.66	7.77	8.88	11.11
95.00	4.21	5.26	6.31	7.36	8.42	10.52
100.00	4.00	5.00	6.00	7.00	8.00	10.00
105.00	3.81	4.76	5.71	6.66	7.61	9.52
110.00	3.64	4.54	5.45	6.36	7.27	9.09
115.00	3.48	4.34	5.21	6.08	6.95	8.69
120.00	3.33	4.16	5.00	5.83	6.66	8.33

TIME IN WHICH A SUM WILL DOUBLE ITSELF.

Rate	Simple Interest	Compound Interest
2 per cent	50 years,	35 years 1 day
3 "	33 years 4 months	23 years 164 days
4 "	25 years,	17 years 246 days
5 "	20 years,	14 years 75 days
6 "	16 years 8 months	11 years 327 days
8 "	12 years 6 months	9 years 2 days
10 "	10 years,	7 years 100 days

Invoice. Merchandise received by the consignee. A Bill. Statement of account forwarded to the consignee or purchaser, itemizing the quantity, prices, charges, etc., of the merchandise sent.

I.O.U. I Owe You.

Ipse Dixit. He himself said it.

Joint Account. A bank account, or other interest in common in the name of two or more parties.

Judgment. A decision of law pronounced by a court enforcing a contract or redressing a wrong.

Judgment Debtor. The one against whom judgment is secured; the debtor. Defendant.

Kilowatt. Measure of electricity. 1,000 watts.

Knot. The statute knot is 6,082.66 feet, and is generally considered the Standard. The number of feet in a knot is arrived at as follows: The circumference of the earth is divided into 360 degrees, each degree containing 60 knots or (360 x 60) 21,600 knots to the circumference. 21,600 divided into 131,385,456 equals the number of feet in the earth's circumference—gives 6,082 feet—the length of a statute knot.

1 knot —1.151 miles   5 knots— 5.757 miles
2 knots—2.303 miles   10 knots—11.515 miles
3 knots—3.454 miles   20 knots—23.030 miles
4 knots—4.606 miles   25 knots—28.787 miles
6 feet—1 fathom; 600 feet—1 cable; 10 cables —1 knot.

Statute mile 5,280 feet (5/6 of a knot).

Lamb. A novice in the ways of Wall Street. A gambler. A speculator. One who buys stocks at random without knowledge or study of what he is dealing in.

Lawful Money. See *Legal Tender.*

Lease. A contract or agreement for the rental of land or a building. LESSEE—The one to whom a lease is made. (Tenant). LESSOR—The one who makes a lease. (Landlord).

FORM OF LEASE.

This Indenture, *made the* ....,
day of...............*one thousand nine hundred and*...............
Between..
of the..........*part,* Witnesseth, *That the said part*......*of the*
first part ha.... letten, and by these presents do.... grant, demise,
and to farm let, unto the said part......*of the second part*...........
....
with the appurtenances, for the term of...........................
from the...................*day of*...............*one thousand nine*
hundred...................*at the*...................*rent or sum of*
....
to be paid in equal...

And *it is agreed that if any rent shall be due and unpaid, or if default shall be made in any of the covenants herein contained, then it shall be lawful for the said part......of the first part to re-enter the said premises and the same to have again, repossess and enjoy.*

And *the said part.....of the second part do.....covenant to pay to the said part........of the first part the said yearly rent as herein specified.*

And *at the expiration of the said terms the said part.......of the second part will quit and surrender the premises hereby demised, in as good state and condition as reasonable use and wear thereof will permit, damages by the elements excepted.*

And *the said part......of the first part do......covenant that the said part......of the second part, on paying the said yearly rent, and performing the covenants aforesaid, shall and may peaceably and quietly have, hold and enjoy the said demised premises for the term aforesaid.*

In Consideration *of the letting of the premises within mentioned to the within named........................and the sum of one dollar to me paid by the said part.....of the first part do....hereby covenant and agree to and with the part......of the first part above named, and ......legal representatives, that if default shall at any time be made by the said........................in the payment of the rent and the performance of the covenants contained in the within lease on.... part to be paid and performed, that........will well and truly pay the said rent or any arrears thereof that may remain due unto the said part......of the first part, and also all damages that may arise in consequence of the non-performance of said covenants, or either of them, without requiring notice of any such default from the said part....... of the first part...*

Witness *..........hand....and seal....this................day of ....in the year one thousand nine hundred and......*

Witness,

Legal Day.   A legal day ends at 12 p. m.

Legal Rate.   See *Interest.*

Legal Tender.   (Or Lawful Money). Gold and silver coins and United States Treasury Notes.

Legend.   The explanation of colors or tracings on a map. Symbols used for indexing. A key.

MAP LEGEND.

Letters of Administration.   Instrument granted by the Court to certain persons who are entitled (preference being given to next of kin) to distribute the estate of a deceased who has left no will.

FORM OF LETTER OF ADMINISTRATION.

The People of the State of New York, *TO.....................*

..deccased, Send Greeting:

Whereas *the said deceased, at the time of.......death, was.......
by means whereof the ordering and granting administration of all and
singular the goods, chattels and credits of the said deceased, and also
the auditing, allowing and final discharging the account thereof, doth
appertain unto us; and we being desirous that the said goods, chattels and credits may be well and faithfully administered, applied and
disposed of, do grant unto you the said*

full power by these presents, to administer and faithfully dispose of all and singular, the said goods, chattels and credits; to ask, demand, recover and receive the debts which unto the said deceased whilst living, and at the time of..........death, did belong; and to pay the debts which the said deceased did owe, so far as such goods, chattels and credits will thereto extend, and the law require: hereby requiring you to make, or cause to be made, a true and perfect inventory of all and singular the goods, chattels and credits of the said deceased, which shall or have come to your hands, possession or knowledge; and the same so made to exhibit, or cause to be exhibited, into the office of the Surrogate of the said County, at or before the expiration of three months from the date hereof, and that you obey all orders of the said Surrogate touching the administration, of the said estate, and render a just and true account of administration, when thereunto required: And we do by these presents depute, constitute and appoint you the said .... Administrat.................of all and singular the goods, chattels and credits which were of the said deceased.

In Testimony whereof, *we have caused the seal of office of our said Surrogate to be hereunto affixed.*

Witness, *...........Surrogate of the said County, at his office in the.......................day of.......................in the year of our Lord one thousand nine hundred..............*

Letters Testa- An instrument issued by the court to the
mentary. Executor (or Executrix) of a will after all
the details incidental to the probating of the
will have been reviewed by the court.

Letter A letter from one bank to its correspondent
of Credit. in another country requesting that the client
to whom the Letter of Credit has been sold,
be furnished with the amount of money or credit stated in

the Letter, the payment of which it guarantees.   See *Travellers Checks.*

CIRCULAR LETTER OF CREDIT
No. T. H. B. 2134

The Statetown Bank

Gentlemen ·   *New York.* _____ *19___*

This will serve to introduce to you and to recommend to your courteous consideration M_____

to whom you will please furnish such funds as_____ may require up to the aggregate amount of L_____

_____Pounds Sterling

against_____demand draft on

THE CITY BANK LIMITED. LONDON

Each draft must be plainly marked as drawn under The Statetown Bank Letter of Credit. No._____and we engage that such drafts shall meet with due honor in London if negotiated on or before

_____19___

The amount of each draft must be entered on the back of this letter and to this we wish to call your special attention.

This Letter of Credit must be cancelled when exhausted and attached to the final draft drawn.   Please see to it that the drafts are signed in your presence, and carefully compare the signature with the specimen below.

Thanking you in anticipation for the attention you may extend to M_____we are,

Very respectfully yours,

To the Bankers mentioned in   _____ PRESIDENT
our List of Correspondents.   _____ CASHIER

Signature of_____

FORM OF LETTER OF CREDIT.

Letter Writing. The remarks that follow are designed to refer only to typewritten business letters.

There may be said to be nine component parts to a letter.

(1) HEADING	**STONE & STONE** 155 WALL STREET NEW YORK
(2) DATE ,.........	December 22, 1916.
(3) ADDRESS	Mr. T. Smith, 103 West Street, New York, N. Y. [Personal]
(4) SALUTATION	Dear Sir:
(5) BODY	Your letter of the 20th instant received this morning. I shall submit the matter to the Chief of Engineers at once, and urge the importance of this work's being gotten under way at the earliest moment possible.
(6) COMPLIMENTARY CLOSE.	With the compliments of the season, I remain,
	Very truly yours,
(7) SIGNATURE	H. G. Jones.
(8) POSTSCRIPT	P.S. Hope to see you at the annual dinner of the Country Club on the 28th.

(9) SUPERSCRIPTION .... Envelope.

(1) Heading (usually printed or engraved)
(2) Date
(3) Address (to whom written)
(4) Salutation (greeting)
(5) Body (paragraphing and divisions)
(6) Complimentary close
(7) Signature
(8) Postscript (if any)
(9) Superscription

(1) HEADING.

Letterheads are usually printed or engraved.   For style of type see *Type*.

A letterhead may include any or all of the following:

> Name of firm
> Nature of business
> Location (state, city, street and number, with room or suite number)
> Telephone number
> Cable address
> Colophon (trademark)
> Officers' names
> Name of department and department head
> In reply refer to file No...... *or* Our File No.
> Address all letters to the firm

The less printing on a letterhead, the more attractive it is.

A typewritten heading should be placed in the upper lefthand corner or the upper center of the blank sheet.

(2) DATE.

Begin date well to the right, so that it ends flush with the righthand margin of the body of the letter.

If not printed on the letterhead, the city and state should appear on the date line.

>Mobile, Ala., August 1, 1916.
>En Route, September 1, 1916.
>En Route East, September 1, 1916.

The traveling member of a firm, while in a distant city, may write letters on the regular letterhead of the firm, on which is printed the address of the home office. In such case, the letter should be dated

>At Texas City, Texas, November 1, 1916.

Except when they precede the months (including instant, ultimo, proximo) *th, st, nd,* or *d* should be omitted after the date number; as,

>November 1, 1916.
>The 12th of December.
>5th instant.

th, st, nd and *d,* not being abbreviations, should not be followed by a period.

The date should be written in full on the *first* page of a letter, not 8/12/16 or 8-12-16; on the second and succeeding pages, figures may be used.

Be careful never to omit the date.

(3) ADDRESS.

In a formal business letter, the address is usually placed at the beginning, although it is not universally so placed.

A friendly business note has the address in the lower lefthand corner.

Forms of Address.

TITLE	ADDRESS	SALUTATION	COMPLIMENTARY CLOSE .
PRESIDENT	President Woodrow Wilson, Executive Mansion, Washington, D. C. To the President of the United States, Washington, D. C. The President, White House, Washington, D. C.	Sir: My dear Mr. President: Mr. President:	I have the honor to be, Yours most respectfully,
EX-PRESIDENT	The Honorable William Howard Taft,	Sir: Dear Sir:	Respectfully yours,
VICE-PRESIDENT ...	To the Vice-President of the United States, Washington, D. C. The Honorable ——— Vice-President of the United States, Washington, D. C. To the President of the Senate, Washington, D. C.	Sir: Dear Sir:	I have the honor to be, Yours most respectfully,
CHIEF JUSTICE.....	Chief Justice of the United States,	Sir: Mr. Chief Justice:	Yours most respectfully,
JUSTICE OF THE SU-PREME OR SUPER-IOR COURT.......	The Hon. ——— Justice of the Supreme Court of the United States, Mr. Justice ———	Sir: Mr. Justice: Dear Mr. Justice ———:	Yours most respectfully,

	Address	Salutation	Complimentary Close
CABINET MEMBER...	The Honorable the Secretary of the Treasury, Hon. William G. McAdoo, Secretary of the Treasury, Washington, D. C.	Sir: Dear Sir:	Yours respectfully, Most respectfully yours,
SENATOR AND CONGRESSMAN.......	The Hon. ——, Senate Office Building, Washington, D. C. The Hon. ——, House Office Building, Washington, D. C. The Hon. ——, M. C., Washington, D. C., (*When not in Washington.*) The Honorable John N. Mitchell, Representative from Texas, Austin, Texas.	Sir: Dear Sir:	Yours most respectfully.
HEADS OF EXECUTIVE DEPARTMENTS AT WASHINGTON...	The Hon. ——	Sir: Dear Sir:	Respectfully,
DIPLOMATS	The Hon. —— (*To Amb. of the U. S. abroad*) His Excellency —— (*To foreign amb. or minister in U. S.*)	Sir: Dear Sir: Your Excellency:	Most respectfully yours,
GOVERNOR	To the Governor of the State of New York, Albany, N. Y. The Honorable —— Governor of the State of Georgia Governor —— His Excellency Gov. ——	Sir: Dear Governor ——: Your Excellency:*	Most respectfully yours.
		("Excellency" is considered un-American*)	

TITLE	ADDRESS	SALUTATION	COMPLIMENTARY CLOSE
LIEUTENANT-GOVERNOR	The Hon. ———	Sir: Dear Sir:	Most respectfully yours,
STATE SENATOR OR REPRESENTATIVE...	The Hon. ———	Dear Sir:	Respectfully,
MAYOR	To the Mayor of Chicago, To the Mayor of the City of Denver, The Hon. John Purroy Mitchel, Mayor of New York City, To His Honor, the Mayor of Buffalo,	Sir: Dear Sir:	Respectfully,
JUDGE	The Hon. ——— (*Name of Court*)	Dear Sir: Sir:	Respectfully,
LAWYER	Stephen S. Smith, Esq..	Dear Sir:	Yours very truly,
POPE	To His Holiness Pope Benedict XV., The Vatican, Rome, Italy. To Our Most Holy Father, Pope Benedict XV., (*"His Holiness" is used in the body of a letter.*)	Most Holy Father: Your Holiness:	Obediently yours: I am, Your Holiness, with profound respect,
CARDINAL	To His Eminence, Cardinal ——— *If also an Archbishop;* His Eminence, ——— Cardinal ———, Archbishop of ——— His Eminence, the Most Reverend ——— Cardinal ———	Your Eminence: Most Eminent and Most Reverend Sir: My Lord Cardinal: Most Eminent Sir:	I have the honor to be, Yours faithfully, With profound respect, I remain, Your obedient servant,

	Address	Salutation	Complimentary Close
ARCHBISHOP	(Anglican) The Most Reverend His Grace, the Archbishop of Canterbury,	My dear Lord Bishop:	I have the honor to remain, Yours faithfully,
	(R. C.) The Most Reverend Archbishop of ——	My Lord:	I have the honor to remain, Yours faithfully,
	The Most Reverend the Archbishop of ——	Most Reverend and dear Sir:	I have the honor to remain, Yours faithfully,
	His Grace the Archbishop of ——	Very Reverend and dear Sir:	
		Your Grace:	
BISHOP	To the Right Reverend —— Bishop of ——	Dear Bishop ——:	Yours sincerely,
	His Lordship the Bishop of ——	My Lord Bishop:	Yours faithfully,
	(R. C.) The Most Reverend A—— B—— Bishop of ——	Reverend and dear Sir:	Yours respectfully,
	The Most Reverend Bishop ——	Most Reverend and dear Sir:	Yours respectfully,
	The Right Reverend Bishop ——	Reverend dear Sir:	Yours respectfully,
		Right Reverend and dear Sir:	
MONSIGNOR	The Right Reverend Monsignor ——	Reverend and dear Monsignor:	Yours faithfully,
		Reverend dear Sir:	Yours respectfully,
MINISTER OR PRIEST	The Reverend A—— B——	Dear Mr. ——:	Yours respectfully,
	(R. C.) The Reverend J—— A——	Reverend Sir:	Yours respectfully,
	Reverend Father ——	Reverend and dear Sir:	Yours respectfully,
		Dear Father A—— ——:	
		Reverend Father:	
BROTHER	Brother Ambrose, —— College,	Very dear Brother:	Yours very truly,
			Yours faithfully,

TITLE	ADDRESS	SALUTATION	COMPLIMENTARY CLOSE
RABBI	The Reverend Abraham Cohn,	Reverend dear Sir:	Yours respectfully,
MOTHER SUPERIOR.	Reverend Mother Alexia, House of Good Shepherd,	Reverend dear Mother: Reverend Mother:	Yours faithfully, Yours respectfully,
	Mother Superior, Academy of the Lady of the Lake,	Dear Reverend Mother:	
	Mother Alexandria, Superior of —— (order)——		
	Mother Alexandria, Superior of —— Sisters of ——		
SISTER	Sister Rose de Lima, St.——	Reverend dear Sister: Dear Sister Rose de Lima: Dear Sister:	Yours respectfully, Yours respectfully,
MARRIED WOMAN...	Mrs. Arthur Jones,	Dear Madam: Madam: Dear Mrs. Jones:	Yours very truly.
UNMARRIED WOMAN.	Miss Elsie Jones,	Dear Madam: My dear Madam: My dear Miss Jones: Dear Miss Jones: Madam: (*Never "Dear Miss:"*)	Yours very truly,
MORE THAN ONE MARRIED WOMAN.	Mesdames Adams & Carey,	Mesdames: Ladies: (*Not "Dear Mesdames:"*)	Yours very truly,
MORE THAN ONE UNMARRIED WOMAN	The Misses A. & L. Carey,	Ladies: Mesdames:	Yours very truly,

Mrs. and Miss....	Mrs. Arthur Jones and Miss Mary Smith,	Dear Madam and Miss: Ladies: Mesdames:	Yours very truly,
Stranger (Woman)	Clara Smith,	Dear Madam:	Yours very truly,
Mr. and Mrs......	Mr. Arthur Jones and Mrs. Walter Smith,	Dear Sir and Madam:	Yours very truly,
Widow	Mrs. Mary Reilly,* (*Or if she prefers to retain her deceased husband's name, providing she has no son bearing his father's name*) Mrs. John Reilly,	Dear Madam:	Yours very truly,
Divorced Woman..	(*If she resumes her full maiden name*) Mrs. Mary Ellen Jones,	Dear Madam:	Yours very truly,
Firm	Frederick A. Stokes Company,	Dear Sirs: Gentlemen:	Yours very truly,
Firm Composed of Men and Women	Paris Costume Company,	Ladies and Gentlemen:	Yours very truly,
Firm of One Woman and Several Men......		*Omit salutation; or use* Dear Sirs:	Yours very truly,
Doctor	Dr. S—— D—— Mrs. S—— D——, M.D.	Dear Sir: Dear Doctor D——:	Yours very truly,
Boy Under Age....	Master Joseph Fagan,	Dear Joseph:	Yours truly,

*Authorities do not agree on this, many preferring Mrs. John Reilly unless the widow herself wishes to be known as Mrs. Mary Reilly.

A title should be placed on the same line with the name.

Mr. James Rutherford, President,
Norfolk Chemical Company,
Norfolk, Va.

not

Mr. James Rutherford,
President Norfolk Chemical Company,
Norfolk, Va.

There has come into vogue among the less conservative typists the style of placing each line of the address flush with the lefthand margin, viz.:

Continental Trust Company,
330 Church Street,
New York City, N. Y.
Dear Sir:

If this style is adopted, it adds to the appearance of a single-spaced letter, and is in better proportion, to begin the paragraphs, also, flush with the lefthand margin, with double spacing between them.

Do not prefix *Messrs.* to a firm name like

The Yates & Earl Company.
George Frost Company.
Frederick A. Stokes Company.

It should be prefixed to the name of a partnership

Messrs. Bell, Polk & Smith.
Messrs. Smith, Jones & Co.

While *Esq.* is commonly used in England, in America it is used entirely according to individual preference.

Many business firms reserve it as a title of compliment or respect for lawyers and distinguished men.

Never use together *Mr.* and *Esq.; Dr.* and *M.D.*

No. or # is not necessary before a street number. A number is obviously a number.

(4) SALUTATION.

My dear Madam is more formal than *Dear Madam.*

Dear Mrs. Jones is less formal than *Dear Madam.*

Dear John or *Dear Elizabeth* is for informal correspondence.

(5) BODY.

Paragraph each new subject.

Paragraph uniformly—one inch from left margin.

If the subject of a letter is given, center it at the top, preferably on the line below the salutation.

Dear Sir:

In re Car Demurrage:

(Note that *re* is not an abbreviation and should have no period after it.)

If more than one subject is covered in the letter, place each subject in large type at the beginning of each paragraph; or if the letter is very long the subjects may be centered.

If writing to a large corporation, and you know the person in charge of the matter under correspondence, write below the address, or center on the line below the salutation—

Attention of Mr. ———

This may also appear on the envelope.

Give your correspondents' file number, when they so request on their letterhead.

In writing to a large company or corporation, when you know the department or official who has charge of the matter you are writing about, make such designation in your address.

> Transportation Department,
> Baltimore and Ohio Railroad,
> Baltimore, Md.

> Receiving Teller,
> Chase National Bank,
> New York, N. Y.

The clever typist, with a little practice, can make the right-hand margin as even as the left, bearing in mind that typewriting is but a form of printing and that by shifting the spaces between words the margins may be made even.

When *Personal, Private* or *Confidential* is placed on the envelope, it also usually appears on the letter.

When a letter is signed with the firm name, be careful to see that the first person plural *we* is used throughout; and similarly, if the letter is signed by an officer of the company, writing in his own name, that *I* is used throughout; if he is speaking or writing *for the firm* we is used; but both we and I should not be used in the same letter.

(6) COMPLIMENTARY CLOSE.

Do not show haste by closing with *Yours,* or worse still, *Yrs.*

When writing to a person of position, a letter of application, or the like, should be closed with *Respectfully yours.*

Cordially yours denotes a friendly personal relation, and is seldom used in business.

Signatures should never be typed. The corporation or firm name when typed may be followed by *Per* or *By* and a signature.

A woman should place *Mrs.* or *Miss* in parenthesis before her name in a business letter or to one who does not know her. (*Miss*) *Margaret Costello.*

A married woman signs *Mary Ellen Smith,* and below, if she is not known to her correspondent, *Mrs. Arthur Smith,* the latter being used in directing the envelope to her.

Flowery and pompous closings such as *I have the honor to remain, my very dear sir,* or *Your obedient, humble servant,* are passé.

Usually the first line of a complimentary close is superfluous and may be dispensed with. When you have concisely and briefly presented the matter, end your letter simply by adding *Yours truly, Yours very truly.*

The first word only is capitalized, and a comma placed at the end of,

> Very respectfully yours,
> Yours truly,
> Yours very truly,
> Very truly yours,
> Respectfully yours,
> Yours respectfully,
> Sincerely yours,
> Yours sincerely,
> Faithfully yours,
> Yours faithfully,
> Yours cordially,

The first line of the complimentary close, if used, should be paragraphed:

> With kind regards, I remain,
>   Yours very truly,
>
> Trusting this meets with your approval, I am,
>   Yours truly,

Use *I am* at the close when there has been no previous correspondence; *I remain,* when there has.

(7) SIGNATURE.

Should always be written.

Should be legibly written, especially if the name does not appear on the printed letterhead. It is a worn-out theory that illegible writing denotes genius. Write plainly; cut out curls, frills and shadings in business letter-writing.

Be careful not to send a letter out without a signature.

A title should never be used in the signature; as John B. Walker, not Professor John B. Walker.

(8) POSTSCRIPT.

Indicates something forgotten, or something to be emphasized.

Should begin as a new paragraph.

Should be signed with initials only. Some business houses dispense with even those.

(9) SUPERSCRIPTION.

(Envelope.)

Direction usually occupies three lines—sometimes four, never two—placed in the center of the envelope.

1—Name
2—Street and number
3—City and state.

The words *street, avenue* and the name of the state may be abbreviated.

No. or # before the street number is superfluous.

If to a large town, always give the street and number; if to a small town, give the county, box or R.F.D. number.

When writing to a large concern, address your letter to the official or department directly in charge of the matter under correspondence.

Attention of Mr. ....
Traffic Department

If the address contains more than three lines, these particular designations may be placed in the lower lefthand corner of the envelope.

The suite or room number may be placed in the lower lefthand corner, if it is desired to augment the address.

If a building instead of a street number be given, it may be written thus:

300 Press Building

Besides the direction, there may be written in the lower lefthand corner any of the following:

Personal	Messenger
Private	Deliver
Confidential	Introducing Miss Blank
Please forward	Kindness of
Transient	Courtesy of
Hold	Favored by
Present	

A letter delivered to another in the same building may be directed

Messrs. Stone & Davis,
BUILDING.

If *The* is part of the firm name, do not prefix *Messrs.*; as,

The R. D. Jones Company.
Messrs. R. D. Jones & Company.

or

Messrs. Thomas A. Strauss & Company.
Thomas A. Strauss Company.

When the name of the street is a number, it should be written out, to avoid juxtaposition of numbers; as,

300 Thirtieth Street.

When north, south, east or west intervenes, it is not necessary to write out; as,

8 West 80th Street.

Envelopes should never be of so poor a quality as to admit of reading part of a letter through them,' nor so poorly gummed as to have the letter received unsealed at its destination, nor of a quality so poor they become torn in the mails.

It is a disgusting habit, and very dangerous to health, to "lick" an envelope to seal it. There are many devices on the market, cheap and cleanly, that may be substituted.

It is undignified to have too much advertising matter appear on the envelope.

A return card may be placed in the upper lefthand corner, e.g.,

Return in........days to
Box........
San Antonio,   Texas.

Or simply the name and address may be used.

If there is no return card in the envelope and the addressee cannot be found, it is sent to the Dead Letter Office. See *Postal.*

Put the stamp on straight, in the upper righthand corner.

Lick the envelope, not the stamp.

Personal may also be written across the back flap of the envelope after it has been sealed, to guard against its being inadvertently opened, while face-down, by other than the person for whom it is intended.

It is a wise precaution to open envelopes, using an envelope-opener, by cutting around three sides, thus laying the envelope entirely open and averting any possibility of the envelope's being thrown away without all of the contents having been removed.

GENERAL.

Business letters should be formal and brief.

Enclosures should be attached to the letter.

If the enclosures are to go with the letter, note in the lower lefthand corner how many.

(Enc.)
(2 Enc.)

It is discourteous to send enclosures without an accompanying note or comment.

It is a hard and fast rule never to write on but one side of the paper in business correspondence.

Intimate letters, or letters of a private nature, should not be typed.

Letters should be promptly acknowledged.

A letter received written in the third person, should be answered in the third person.

When acknowledging receipt of a letter, refer first to its date, and follow with a brief summary of what it contained.

Acknowledge a check promptly, referring to its date and number.

Return postage should be enclosed in letters about one's own affairs when a reply is desired.

Don't typewrite your signature; don't write your signature with a pencil; use pen and ink.

Don't forget to date your letter.

Don't use ruled paper for typewritten letters.

Don't send a typewritten letter except on business.

Too much underscoring weakens rather than strengthens a letter.

The initials of the dictator are placed at the lower left-hand. It is not usual nor dignified to place the initials of the president or superior officer on the letter, as the purpose of placing the dictator's and typist's initials on the letter is to show the president or head of the firm which one of his employees is responsible for or has charge of the matter under correspondence.

The initials of the full name of the dictator and the last name of the typist is the usual style.

JHS-R   ABW/O   R.W.C.
K

Quoted matter is usually centered and single-spaced. (As a telegram.)

We speak of "addressing the letter" and "directing the envelope."

Fold a large letterhead up to within a quarter-inch of the top, then in thirds.

There are many devices for sealing envelopes. They should never be sealed with the tongue: should one have a cut or abrasion on the lip, it might result disastrously.

Postals or postcards should contain no salutation or complimentary close—simply dated and signed with initials. It goes without saying that no private, confidential or offensive matter should ever be sent on postcards.

See *Postage*.

Formal Letter of Recommendation.

Should not be sealed.

New York, Oct. 1, 1916.

To Whom It May Concern:

This is to certify that the bearer, Miss Blank, has been in our employ five years as statistician, in which capacity she has given complete satisfaction.

(Signature.)

Combined Letter of Introduction and Recommendation.

A letter of introduction, when to be presented, should not be sealed.

Newark, N. J., Oct. 1, 1916.

Mr. F. W. Corey, President,
Union Trust Company,
Newark, N. J.

Dear Mr. Corey:

This will introduce to you the bearer, Miss Blank, who desires to apply for the position of Private Secretary which, at my request, you so kindly have held open until today.

I can speak only in the highest terms of Miss Blank's character and ability.

Yours very truly,

JOHN R. ROWE.

The envelope should bear the name and address of the person to whom it is directed, just as if sent by mail, and in the lower lefthand corner—

Introducing Miss Blank

It is courteous to acknowledge a letter of introduction.

Liabilities.　See *Assets and Liabilities.*

Lien.　　An indebtedness, right, title or claim. A mortgage is a LIEN.

MECHANICS LIEN—The claim of mechanics or laborers for construction work that has been finished but not paid for.

Life Insurance.　A life insurance policy does not take effect until the first premium is paid. Failure to pay premiums voids the policy.

In case the person insured commits suicide, or dies by the hand of the law or of crime, the insurance company is not liable, but if the insured should kill himself while in-sane the policy would still be valid.

The rates for life insurance vary with the age of the in-dividual. These rates are calculated by the official statisti-cian of the insurance company, who is called the actuary. The rate, or commission, paid for the insurance is called the premium.

The insurance company makes a physical examination before accepting the application for life insurance and applicants should answer all questions to the very best of their knowledge. However, a slight, unintentional dis-crepancy does not invalidate a policy.

Limitation, Statutes of. See *Debts.*

Limited— Ltd. See *Partnership.*

Lis Pendens. Notice of a pending suit.

Listed Securities. Securities permitted to be dealt in on a stock exchange. See *Stock Exchange.*

From report of the Hughes Commission on the N. Y. Stock Exchange, dated July 7, 1909: "Before securities can be bought and sold on the Exchange, they must be examined. The committee on Stock List is one of the most important parts of the organization, since public confidence depends upon the honesty, impartiality, and thoroughness of its work. While the Exchange does not guarantee the character of any securities, or affirm that the statements filed by the promoters are true, it certifies that due diligence and caution have been used by experienced men in examining them. Admission to the list, therefore, establishes a presumption in favor of the soundness of the security so admitted.''

Lloyds. A set of English underwriters or subscribers to marine insurance. When insurance is desired on a vessel or cargo against loss or damage at sea, the RISK is offered to the underwriters, who accept it at a specified premium, or decline it. The risk is usually divided among the underwriters. LLOYDS also distributes authentic information to shippers all over the world.

Log. A ship's diary.

1915.

July 16th Left Port.......12:25 with Barge............ for southerly end of channel, returning to dock 2:34 p. m.

17th 7:30 a. m. went to Jackson's wharf, took five tons water, returning to dock 1 p. m.

18th Left for Key West with Barge...........7 a. m.

EXTRACT FROM LOG OF A TUG BOAT.

Long and Short. (Finance) LONG—A speculator who has bought stocks—a ''Bull''; SHORT—A speculator who has sold—a ''Bear''.

Manifest. A schedule or list of the cargo or passengers on a ship.

Manifest, of part of Cargo Shipped by..on board the........................

whereof........................is Master (or Conductor), for........................

New York,........................19   ☞ See instructions on the other side.

MARKS	NUMBERS	PACKAGES AND CONTENTS With Articles Fully Described	Quantities Lbs., Gallons, &c.	No. 1 Value of Domestic Merchandise	No. 2 Value of Foreign Merchandise "Free of Duty"	No. 3 Value of Foreign Merchandise from Bonded Warehouse	No. 4 Value of Foreign Merchandise not from Bonded Warehouse which has paid duties	No. 5 Value of Foreign Merchandise "In Transit" through the United States	TO BE LANDED AT—

FORM OF SHIPPER'S MANIFEST, PART-OF-CARGO.

DISTRICT AND PORT OF NEW YORK:

I, ..., do solemnly, sincerely and truly swear, that the within manifest contains a full, just and true account of all the Goods, Wares and Merchandise shipped by..............................., on board the within named vessel (or vehicle), and that the quantities and values of each article are truly stated, according to their actual cost or the values which they truly bear in this Port at this time.

And I further swear that the said merchandise is truly intended to be exported to

....

....

....

So HELP ME GOD.

Sworn to, this.............................19

before me,

....

Collector.

INSTRUCTIONS.

Column No. 1 shall embrace all *domestic merchandise,* whether exported "in bond" under the internal-revenue act, or otherwise; and also all manufactures from foreign products, such as sugar refined from foreign sugar, coffee and spices having been ground or adulterated, etc., whether exported with benefit of drawback or not.

Column No. 2 shall embrace all *foreign merchandise* "free of duty."

Column No. 3 shall embrace all *foreign merchandise* exported from "bonded warehouse," duties remaining unpaid, or which, having been paid, are returnable as drawback.

Column No. 4 shall embrace all *foreign merchandise* on which the duties have been paid, and which has left the custody of the officers of the customs, provided the condition of the merchandise has not been changed. If manufactured, adulterated, or changed in any manner, it becomes domestic merchandise, and must be classified as such.

Column No. 5 shall embrace all *foreign merchandise* "in transit" through the United States.

Specify all merchandise in specific and not general terms. Do not use "fruit" for apples, oranges, prunes, etc., when green, ripe, or dried, but if preserved the general term "preserved fruit" may be used, but it must be stated whether "in cans" or "not in cans;" nor "groceries" for tea, coffee, spices sugar, molasses, etc.; nor "provisions" for hams, bacon, lard, etc.; nor "vegetables" for beans, onions, potatoes, etc., when fresh or dried, but when canned the general term "canned vegetables" may be used; nor "canned goods" for canned vegetables, canned beef, canned salmon, etc.; nor "meat" for beef, mutton, pork, etc.; nor "hardware" unless it covers locks, hinges, fastenings, or other builders' hardware, but specify separately the articles, such as tools, saws, kitchen utensils, cutlery, etc.; nor "machinery" or "machines," but state the kind, whether electrical, printing presses, pumps, typewriters, etc., nor "animals" for horses, mules, cattle, hogs, etc.; nor any other general term but specify the merchandise in detail according to each particular kind.

In the case of cheese be particular to state whether filled or unfilled; butter, whether pure, adulterated, or renovated; and oleomargarine, whether colored or uncolored. If adulterated or renovated butter (called also "process" butter), shippers must present at the custom-house with this manifest a certificate of purity issued by the United States inspector of dairy exports.

Specify "quantities" in all cases whenever possible. State the kind of package, whether box, chest, case, bale, cask, etc.

The face of the manifest will conform to that prescribed in article 129 of the same regulations, for the masters of vessels, except that the title of the column headed, "Packages and contents or articles in bulk" will be changed to read, "Packages and contents with articles fully described."

Article 130, regulations of 1899, is hereby amended.

Maintenance of Equipment. A railroad term used in reporting the cost of repairs to or up-keep of locomotives, passenger cars, freight cars, shop machinery, and tools, power plant, etc., etc.

Maintenance of Ways and Structures. A railroad term used in reporting the amounts expended for the up-keep of the roadway and buildings, embracing such items as Superintendence; ballast; ties; rails; track material; removal of snow, sand and ice; tunnels; bridges and trestles; culverts; over and undergrade crossings; grade crossings, fences, cattle guards and signs; snow and sand fences and snowsheds; signal and interlocking plants; telegraph and telephone lines; electric power transmission; buildings, fixtures and grounds; docks and wharves; roadway tools and supplies; injuries to persons; stationery and printing, and other expenses.

Mandamus. The command of a court.

Margin. An allowance or additional amount set aside to meet unforeseen conditions.

The difference between the price at which an article is purchased and the price at which it is sold after providing for expenses and profit.

Money or securities deposited with the lender in excess of the loan.

Dealing on MARGIN is the speculating on the rise or fall in the prices of securities. If, for example, one share of stock is being dealt in, the broker would require 10% of the par value of the stock to be deposited with him (more than 10% is required for stocks that have a doubtful market or that fluctuate to any great extent). If the par value is $100., say, the broker requires $10. on deposit, from which is deducted his commissions and interest. Assuming these to amount to $3., there remain $7. margin to work on. When the fluctuation in the price of the stock absorbs this $7., more *margin* is demanded or the account closed out. See *Bulls and Bears, Long and Short.*

Marine Insurance. Insurance on steamers, boats, and their cargoes.

Maritime Exchange. Located in its own building on Broad Street, N. Y. City. Membership consists of those interested in the shipping trade.

Mark. See *Coins, Foreign Value of.*

Maturity. Due date of notes, bills, bonds, etc.

Merger. The absorption of one company by another. A combination of one or more companies.

Mileage. A passenger rate per mile.

Money Orders. Postal money orders are issued for any desired amount from 1 cent to $100. When a larger sum than $100. is to be sent, additional orders can be obtained. Fees for money orders payable in the United States (which includes Hawaii and Porto Rico) and its possessions, comprising the Canal Zone, Guam, the Philippines, and Tutuila, Samoa; also for

orders payable in Bermuda, British Guiana, British Hon-
duras, Canada, Cuba, Mexico, Newfoundland, at the
United States Postal Agency at Shanghai (China), in the
Bahama Islands and in certain other islands in the West
Indies are as follows:

```
For orders from $ 0.01 to $ 2.50.................. 3 cents
         from    2.50 to    5.00.................. 5 cents
         from    5.01 to   10.00.................. 8 cents
         from   10.01 to   20.00..................10 cents
         from   20.01 to   30.00..................12 cents
         from   30.01 to   40.00..................15 cents
         from   40.01 to   50.00..................18 cents
         from   50.01 to   60.00..................20 cents
         from   60.01 to   75.00..................25 cents
         from   75.01 to  100.00..................30 cents
```

A money order drawn in favor of a person residing on
a rural route may be paid through the carrier if entrusted
to him for collection, with a written request addressed to
the postmaster that payment be so made.

The person presenting a money order for payment, or
making inquiry relative thereto, will, if unknown, be required to prove his identity before payment will be made,
or information concerning the order be given.

More than one indorsement on a money order is prohibited, but additional signatures may be affixed for the
purpose of identifying the payee or indorsee, or of guar-
anteeing his signature.

A domestic order which has not been paid within one
year from the last day of the month of its issue is invalid,
but the owner may secure payment of the amount by making application to the Postal Department through the
postmaster at any money order office.

When a domestic money order has been lost, the owner
may, upon application to the postmaster at any money

order office, obtain a duplicate to be issued in its stead within one year from the last day of the month of issue.

EXPRESS money orders upon proper identification will be cashed by any agent of the express company. The rates are the same as for Postal money orders.

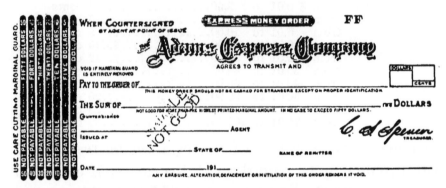

REDUCED FACSIMILE OF EXPRESS MONEY ORDER.

MONEY TRANSFERRED BY TELEGRAPH—The charges for sending money by telegraph between points in the United States are as follows:

$25 or less.. 25c.
Over $25 and not exceeding $50...................... 35c.
Over $50 and not exceeding $75...................... 60c.
Over $75 and not exceeding $100..................... 85c.
For each $100 or fraction thereof up to $3,000........ 25c.
For each $100 or fraction thereof over $3,000........ 20c.

In addition to the premium, charge for telegraph service the tolls, at regular day rates, on one (15) word message between transfer points.

Examples:

The premium for a transfer of $125 will be 85c. for $100 and 25c. for the additional $25, total $1.10.

For $3,000 the premium will be 85c. for $100 and 25c. for each additional $100, or a total of $8.10.

For $3,500 the premium will be $8.10 for $3,000 and 20c. for each additional $100, or a total of $9.10.

Any fractional part of a dollar will be counted as a dollar.

Money may be sent by Telegraph and Cable to all parts of the world.

Mortgage. A document under seal, whereunder the mortgagor (borrower) transfers to the mortgagee (lender) certain described property to be held as security until payment of the debt. A wife should also sign.

FORM OF MORTGAGE, INT., TAX, ASSESS. AND WARRANTY—GREATER NEW YORK.

INDIVIDUAL TO INDIVIDUAL OR CORPORATION.

𝕿𝖍𝖎𝖘 𝕴𝖓𝖉𝖊𝖓𝖙𝖚𝖗𝖊, *made the.. day of...................., in the year nineteen hundred and......*

𝕭𝖊𝖙𝖜𝖊𝖊𝖓 *... ....part.....of the first part and ....part.....of the second part,*

𝖂𝖍𝖊𝖗𝖊𝖆𝖘, *the said.. ....justly indebted to the said part....of the second part in the sum of..................................lawful money of the United States, secured to be paid by.....................certain bond or obligation bearing even date herewith, conditioned for the payment of the said sum of... on the............day of.................nineteen hundred and.... and the interest thereon, to be computed from the day of the date of this Indenture at the rate of.............................per centum per annum and to be paid...*

𝕴𝖙 𝖇𝖊𝖎𝖓𝖌 𝖙𝖍𝖊𝖗𝖊𝖇𝖞 𝖊𝖝𝖕𝖗𝖊𝖘𝖘𝖑𝖞 𝖆𝖌𝖗𝖊𝖊𝖉, *that the whole of the said principal sum shall become due after default in the payment of interest, taxes or assessments, as hereinafter provided.*

𝕹𝖔𝖜 𝖙𝖍𝖎𝖘 𝕴𝖓𝖉𝖊𝖓𝖙𝖚𝖗𝖊 𝖂𝖎𝖙𝖓𝖊𝖘𝖘𝖊𝖙𝖍, *that the said part....of the first part, for the better securing the payment of the said sum of money mentioned in the condition of the said bond or obligation, with interest thereon, and also for and in consideration of one dollar paid by the said part....of the second part, the receipt whereof is hereby acknowledged, do.....hereby grant and release unto the said part.....of the second part and to...heirs and assigns, forever,*

𝕬𝖑𝖑

𝕿𝖔𝖌𝖊𝖙𝖍𝖊𝖗 *with the appurtenances and all the estate and rights of the said part....of the first part in and to said premises.*

To have and to hold, *the above granted premises unto the said part.... of the second part,..*
and assigns, forever, ...

Provided Always, *that if the said part.....of the first part.......*
heirs, executors or administrators, shall pay unto the said part.....of the second part..
or assigns, the said sum of money mentioned in the condition of the said bond or obligation and the interest thereon at the time and in the manner mentioned in the said condition that then these presents and the estate hereby granted, shall cease, determine and be void.

And *the said...*
the said part....of the first part covenant....with the part....of the second part as follows:
First—That ....
the part....of the first part will pay the indebtedness as hereinbefore provided, and if default be made in the payment of any part thereof of the part.....of the second part shall have power to sell the premises herein described, according to law.
Second—And it is hereby expressly agreed that the whole of said principal sum shall become due at the option of the said part....of the second part after default in the payment of any installment of principal or of interest for.............days, or after default in the payment of any tax or assessment.................for...........days after notice and demand.
Third—That ....
the part.....of the first part will execute any further necessary assurance of the title to said premises and will forever warrant said title.

In Witness Whereof, *the said part......of the first part ha.....*
hereunto set...........hand.....and seal......the day and year first above written.

In Presence of

When the mortgagor defaults in the payment of either principal or interest, the mortgage can be foreclosed in accordance with the conditions of the mortgage, the property sold and the mortgage satisfied from the proceeds of sale.

CHATTEL MORTGAGE—A transfer of the title to movable or personal property, such as household furniture.

Short Form of Chattel Mortgage.

Know all Men by these Presents, *that I..................... of the town of....................county of........................ being indebted to...in the sum of ....dollars, with interest from this date, for the security of said sum, I do hereby mortgage, sell and assign to the said...all the goods and chattels of every kind and description now in the dwelling-house situated .... in the town of......................., and I do hereby authorize and empower the said...........................to take possession of said goods and chattels on default in the payment of the said indebtedness on and after the........day of.....................19..., and to sell the same and to apply the proceeds of such sale to the payment of said debt and interest, the surplus (if any) to be paid over to me.*

In Witness Whereof, *I have hereunto set my hand and seal this ....day of........................19...*

SECOND MORTGAGE—Subsidiary to the prior or first mortgage.

BLANKET MORTGAGE—A mortgage covering several pieces of property. Sometimes called a General Mortgage.

As soon as possible after the execution of a mortgage it should be recorded in the office of the County Clerk or Register's office.

See *Assignment.*

Municipals. Bonds issued by a village, township, city, county, state or territory.

Naturaliza- To BECOME A CITIZEN, an alien shall, at
tion. least two years prior to his admission to citizenship and after he has reached the age of 18 years, DECLARE HIS INTENTION, under oath, to become a citizen of the United States.

132

DECLARATION OF INTENTION.

(INVALID FOR ALL PURPOSES SEVEN (7) YEARS AFTER THE DATE HEREOF.)

STATE OF...................... ⎫
                              ⎬ *ss.:*
COUNTY OF.................... ⎭

In the ....Court

of ....

I.......................................*aged......years, occupation*
...............................*do* declare on oath *that my personal*
                                    affirm
*description is: Color......... Complexion..........height..........
feet.........inches, weight............pounds, color of hair..........
color of eyes............other visible distinctive marks.............;
I was born in...................on the........day of..........1....
I now reside at.......................... I emigrated to the United
States of America from................on the vessel...............;
my last foreign residence was.................... It is my bona fide
intention to renounce forever all allegiance and fidelity to any foreign
prince, potentate, state or sovereignty, and particularly to.............
................of which I am now a citizen (subject); I arrived at*
                                                        State
the port of......................in the Territory of................
                                        District
*on or about the...........day of...................1...; I am not an
anarchist; I am not a polygamist nor a believer in the practice of
polygamy; and it is my intention in good faith to become a citizen of the
United States of America and to permanently reside therein; So Help
Me God.*

....

(SEAL)

Subscribed and sworn to *before me this............*
                  affirmed
day of ....anno Domini......1....

....

Clerk of the................Court.

No alien can be naturalized or admitted as a CITIZEN of the U. S. who cannot speak the English language, but this does not prevent him from taking the first papers.

He shall reside in the United States at least FIVE YEARS prior to the date of his application for citizenship, and within the state or territory ONE YEAR, and two witnesses shall make affidavit to these facts and that the applicant is of good moral character; and he must be 21 years of age.

White persons and those of the African race only admitted to citizenship.

Naturalization of alien enemies prohibited.

Must be a believer in organized government, not a polygamist, and must state he will support the Constitution of the United States.

Must forever renounce all allegiance and fidelity to any foreign prince, potentate, state or sovereignty.

Shall renounce any title or order of nobility.

Any woman married to a citizen of the U. S. and who might herself be lawfully naturalized shall be deemed a citizen.

Any American woman who marries a foreigner shall take the nationality of her husband.

Any foreign woman who marries an American shall be assumed to retain her American citizenship even after the termination of the marital relations if she continue to reside in the United States.

Article XIV, adopted as an amendment to the Constitution of the U. S. in 1868, provides: "All persons born or naturalized in the United States, and subject to the jurisdiction thereof, are citizens of the United States and of the state wherein they reside. No state shall make or enforce any law which shall abridge the privileges or immunities of citizens of the United States; nor shall any state deprive any person of life, liberty or property without due process of law, nor deny to any person within its jurisdiction the equal protection of the laws.''

Negotiable Instruments. Those instruments that may be passed from hand to hand and used in payment of debts. The ''Negotiable Instrument Law,'' in effect in most of the states, covers bills of exchange, notes, checks, drafts, bills of lading, etc.

Nil. Nothing.

Notary Public. An officer appointed by the state with authority to attest papers, protest commercial paper, administer oaths, take acknowledgments, etc. In New York state, any person is eligible (except a public officer) who is a citizen of the United States and a resident of the state with a legal residence in the county for which he or she desires to be appointed, and is 21 years of age or over. Term two years.

LICENSE FEES:

In New York, Kings or Bronx County.............$10.00
In a city of more than 50,000 and less than 600,000... 5.00
Elsewhere in New York State...................... 2.50

Notes. To be negotiable, a Note must be in writing and signed by the maker. It must contain an unconditional promise or order to pay a certain sum in money.   Must be payable on demand or at a fixed future time.   Must be payable to order or to bearer.

```
┌─────────────────────────────────────────────────────────┐
│                                                           │
│  $.....................      NEW YORK,........................19           │
│                                                           │
│  ...........................................MONTHS  AFTER  DATE,  FOR  VALUE   │
│                                                           │
│  RECEIVED,  I  PROMISE  TO  PAY..................................   │
│                                                           │
│  ..................................................................OR  ORDER,  │
│                                                           │
│  .......................................................... DOLLARS       │
│                                                           │
│  WITH  INTEREST.                                          │
│                   ....................................................  │
│                                                           │
└─────────────────────────────────────────────────────────┘
```

FORM OF NEGOTIABLE NOTE.

By endorsing a note, one transfers an instrument and warrants to every subsequent holder that the instrument is genuine, that he has title to it, and that if not paid by the party primarily liable at maturity, he will pay it upon receiving due notice of non-payment.   To hold an endorser liable, the holder, upon its non-payment at maturity, must give prompt notice of such non-payment to the endorser and that the holder looks to the endorser for payment. Such notice should be sent within twenty-four hours. When an endorser is thus compelled to pay he may hold prior parties through whom he received the instrument liable to him by sending them prompt notice of non-payment upon receiving such notice from the holder.   One who transfers a negotiable instrument by delivery, without endorsing it, simply warrants that the instrument is genuine, that he has title to it, and knows of no defense to it, but does not agree to pay it if unpaid at maturity.

The maker of a note is liable to pay it, if unpaid at maturity, without any notice from the holder or indorser. Notice to one of several partners is sufficient notice to all.

A bona fide holder of a negotiable instrument, that is, a party who takes an instrument regular on its face before its maturity pays value for it and has no knowledge of any defence to it, is entitled to hold the party primarily liable responsible for its payment, despite any defence he may have against the party to whom he gave it, except such as rendered the instrument void at its inception. Thus, if the maker of a note received no value for it, or was induced to issue through fraud or imposition, they do not defeat the right of a bona fide holder to compel its payment from him.

A promissory note which makes no mention of interest carries none, but if the note is not paid at maturity, interest is computed at the legal rate from the expiration of the three days grace until the debt is paid.—(*World Almanac.*)

WITHOUT RECOURSE written after the endorsement on a Note relieves the endorser from any liability if the maker does not pay the note.

FORM OF STOCK NOTE.

$............   *New York,*.....................19

.............................*after date, for value received*.....*promise*

to pay to the order of...

.... *Dollars*

with interest at....*per cent. per annum, payable at*..................

having deposited with........*as collateral security for payment of this*

or any other liability or liabilities of........*to said*..............

due or to become due, or that may be hereafter contracted, the following property, viz.:

The market value of which is now $................with the right on the part of said...............from time to time to demand such additional collateral security as.....may deem sufficient should the market value thereof decline, and upon......failure to comply with any such demand, this obligation shall forthwith become due, with full power and authority to........or........assigns in case of such default or of the non-payment of any of the liabilities above mentioned at maturity, to sell, assign and deliver the whole, or any part of such securities or any substitutes therefor or additions thereto at any broker's board or at public or private sale, at their option, at any time or times, thereafter without advertisement or notice to..............and with the right on ....part to become purchasers thereof, at such sale or sales, freed and discharged of any equity of redemption. And after deducting all legal or other costs and expenses for collection, sale and delivery, to apply the residue of the proceeds of such sale or sales so made, to pay any, either or all of said liabilities, as said........................... shall deem proper, returning the overplus to the undersigned; and ....will still remain liable for any amount so unpaid.

Obligation. An indebtedness.

Officers. For duties of officers of a company, see *By-Laws.*

Option. A written or verbal agreement, with or without consideration, between parties, giving one the right to accept or decline a proposition within a time limit; e. g., the prospective purchaser of a piece of land asks an OPTION on it for thirty days, within which time the prospective seller cannot dispose of it to anyone else. Preferential right. A reservation.

```
                                    --------------------191----

For and in consideration of the sum of----------------------------------
to me in hand paid, receipt of which is hereby acknowledged, I----------
------------------------------hereby grant to-----------------------
an option of 90 days from date to buy-------------------------------
-----------------------------------------------------------------
                              ---------------------------------
```

FORM OF OPTION.

Order. A written instruction; mandate of a judge or court.

```
                    New York,---------------------19----------
Mr. T. J. Spencer,
      Please pay Martin Brown or order,
One Hundred Dollars in merchandise and charge
the same to the account of
                                    Walter Smith.
```

FORM OF ORDER FOR GOODS.

Outlawed. See *Notes, Debts.*

Overdraft. See *Checks.*

Par. The nominal value of a stock. Face value.
Stocks are usually issued at a PAR value of
$100., although it may be $5.00, $10.00, or $50.00.

Parcel Post or Fourth Class Matter. Embraces that known as Domestic Parcel Post Mail and includes merchandise, farm and factory products, seeds, cuttings, bulbs, roots, scions and plants, books (including catalogs) miscellaneous printed matter weighing more than four pounds and all other mailable matter not embraced in the first, second and third classes. See *Postage*.

The Domestic Parcel Post offers a convenient, quick, and efficient means of transporting mailable parcels to any post office in the United States and its possessions. The service reaches more places than any other transportation agency. It brings producers and consumers into closer contact, thus opening the way to reducing the high cost of living. Special treatment and advantages are accorded shipments of farm products weighing between 20 and 50 pounds. Parcels may be insured against loss and may be sent C.O.D.

U. S. PARCEL POST RATES.

Parcels weighing 4 ounces or less, except books, seeds, plants, etc., one cent for each ounce or fraction thereof, any distance.

Eight ounces or less containing books, seeds, cuttings, bulbs, roots, scions, and plants, one cent for each two ounces or fraction thereof, regardless of distance.

More than eight ounces, containing books, seeds, plants, etc., parcels of miscellaneous printed matter weighing more than 4 pounds, and all other parcels of fourth-class matter weighing more than four ounces are chargeable, according to distance or zone, at the pound rates shown in

the following table, a fraction of a pound being considered
a full pound.

POUND RATES.

Weight in Pounds	Local	ZONES							
		1st Up to 50 miles	2nd 50 to 150 miles	3rd 150 to 300 miles	4th 300 to 600 miles	5th 600 to 1000 miles	6th 1000 to 1400 miles	7th 1400 to 1800 miles	8th Over 1800 miles
1	$0.05	$0.05	$0.05	$0.06	$0.07	$0.08	$0.09	$0.11	$0.12
2	.06	.06	.06	.08	.11	.14	.17	.21	.24
3	.06	.07	.07	.10	.15	.20	.25	.31	.36
4	.07	.08	.08	.12	.19	.26	.33	.41	.48
5	.07	.09	.09	.14	.23	.32	.41	.51	.60
6	.08	.10	.10	.16	.27	.38	.49	.61	.72
7	.08	.11	.11	.18	.31	.44	.57	.71	.84
8	.09	.12	.12	.20	.35	.50	.65	.81	.96
9	.09	.13	.13	.22	.39	.56	.73	.91	1.08
10	.10	.14	.14	.24	.43	.62	.81	1.01	1.20
11	.10	.15	.15	.26	.47	.68	.89	1.11	1.32
12	.11	.16	.16	.28	.51	.74	.97	1.21	1.44
13	.11	.17	.17	.30	.55	.80	1.05	1.31	1.56
14	.12	.18	.18	.32	.59	.86	1.13	1.41	1.68
15	.12	.19	.19	.34	.63	.92	1.21	1.51	1.80
16	.13	.20	.20	.36	.67	.98	1.29	1.61	1.92
17	.13	.21	.21	.38	.71	1.04	1.37	1.71	2.04
18	.14	.22	.22	.40	.75	1.10	1.45	1.81	2.16
19	.14	.23	.23	.42	.79	1.16	1.53	1.91	2.28
20	.15	.24	.24	.44	.83	1.22	1.61	2.01	2.40
21	.15	.25	.25						
22	.16	.26	.26						
23	.16	.27	.27						
24	.17	.28	.28						
25	.17	.29	.29						
26	.18	.30	.30						
27	.18	.31	.31						
28	.19	.32	.32						
29	.19	.33	.33						
30	.20	.34	.34						
31	.20	.35	.35						
32	.21	.36	.36						
33	.21	.37	.37						
34	.22	.38	.38						
35	.22	.39	.39						
36	.23	.40	.40						
37	.23	.41	.41						
38	.24	.42	.42						
39	.24	.43	.43						
40	.25	.44	.44						
41	.25	.45	.45						
42	.26	.46	.46						
43	.26	.47	.47						
44	.27	.48	.48						
45	.27	.49	.49						
46	.28	.50	.50						
47	.28	.51	.51						
48	.29	.52	.52						
49	.29	.53	.53						
50	.30	.54	.54						

ZONES—PARCEL POST GUIDE AND MAPS.
For parcel post purposes the United States is divided
into units of area thirty minutes square. Such units
form the basis of the eight postal zones. To ascertain in
which zone a post office is located from the office of mailing, a parcel post guide, costing 55 cents, and map,
costing 20 cents, are jointly used. The guide applies to
all offices, but a separate map is required for each unit.
A zone key is furnished with the guide for use in the
units of area in which some of the largest post offices
are located, and makes the map for those units unneces-
sary. The guide and maps may be purchased by sending
a money order to the Third Assistant Postmaster General, Washington, D. C. Stamps are not accepted.

The limit of weight of fourth-class matter is 50 pounds
for parcels mailed for delivery within the first and second

zones, and 20 pounds for all other zones. (Subject to change).

The size of a parcel may not exceed 72 inches in length and girth combined. In measuring a parcel, the greatest distance in a straight line between the ends (but not around the parcel) is taken as its length, while the distance around the parcel at its thickest part is taken as its girth. For example, a parcel 35 inches long, 10 inches wide, and 5 inches high measures 65 inches in length and girth combined.

A parcel of fourth-class matter will not be accepted for mailing UNLESS IT BEARS THE NAME AND ADDRESS OF THE SENDER, which should be preceded by the word "FROM."

Ordinary or parcel post stamps are valid.

Parcels subject to Zone rates must be mailed at the General Post Office or a branch.

Parcels must be prepared for mailing in such manner that the contents can be easily examined.

Parcel-post matter can not be registered, but may be insured against loss upon payment of small fee.

Parcel-post packages may be sent "Special Delivery."

Envelopes of weak or unsubstantial paper should not be used.

Harmful articles not absolutely excluded from the mails, but which, from their form or nature, might, unless properly secured, destroy, deface or otherwise damage the contents of the mail bag, or harm the person of anyone engaged in the postal service, may be transmitted in the mails only when packed in accordance with postal regulations.

Partnership. An alliance between two or more persons who agree to invest their time, labor and means, sharing the profit or loss that may be the outcome of the enterprise.

"Limited" partnership or company is one wherein the liability of the members or shareholders for the debts of the company is limited to an amount equalling the shares they hold or capital they have put in. A company whose liabilities are limited to the amount of its capital stock.

FORM OF ARTICLES OF CO-PARTNERSHIP.

Article of Agreement, *made the........day of.............*
one thousand nine hundred and....................................
Between ....
party of the first part, and
party of the second part, as follows, ...
The said parties above named have agreed to become co-partners in
business, ...
and by these presents do agree to be co-partners together under and by
the name or firm of·..
in the buying, selling and vending of all sorts of goods, wares and mer-
chandise to the said business belonging, and to occupy the............
their co-partnership to commence on the...........day of.............
19..., and to continue..
..
and to that end and purpose the said................................
..
to be used and employed in common between them for the support and
management of the said business, to their mutual benefit and advantage.

And *it is agreed by and between the parties to these presents that at*
all times during the continuance of their co-partnership, they and each
of them will give their attendance, and do their and each of their best
endeavors, and to the utmost of their skill and power exert themselves
for their joint interest, profit, benefit and advantage, and truly employ,
buy, sell, and merchandise with their joint stock, and the increase there-
of, in the business aforesaid.

And also *that they shall and will at all times during the said co-*
partnership, bear, pay, and discharge equally between them, all rents,

and other expenses that may be required for the support and management of the said business; and that all gains, profit and increase that shall come, grow or arise from or by means of their said business, shall be divided between them, and all loss that shall happen to their joint business by ill commodities, bad debts or otherwise, shall be borne and paid between them.

And it is agreed by and between the said parties, that there shall be had and kept at all times during the continuance of their co-partnership, perfect, just, and true books of account, wherein each of the said co-partners shall enter and set down as well all money by them or either of them received, paid, laid out and expended in and about the said business, as also all goods, wares, commodities and merchandise, by them or either of them bought or sold, by reason or on account of the said business, and all other matters and things whatsoever, to the said business and the management thereof in anywise belonging; which said book shall be used in common between the said co-partners, so that either of them may have access thereto, without any interruption or hindrance of the other.

And also, the said co-partners, once in............................ or oftener if necessary, shall make, yield and render, each to the other, a true, just, and perfect inventory and account of all profits and increase by them, or either of them, made, and all losses by them, or either of them, sustained; and also all payments, receipts, disbursements and all other things by them made, received, disbursed, acted, done, or suffered in this said co-partnership and business; and the same account so made shall and will clear, adjust, pay and deliver, each to the other, at the time their just share of the profits so made as aforesaid.

And the said parties hereby mutually covenant and agree, to and with each other, that during the continuance of the said co-partnership, neither of them shall nor will endorse any note, or otherwise become surety for any person or persons whomsoever, without consent of the other of the said co-partners. And at the end or other sooner termination of their co-partnership the said co-partners, each to the other, shall and will make a true, just and final account of all things relating to their said business, and in all things truly adjust the same; and all and every the stock and stocks, as well as the gains and increase thereof, which shall appear to be remaining, either in money, goods, wares, fixtures, debts or otherwise, shall be divided between them.

A partnership may be dissolved in accordance with the Articles of Co-partnership, by the death or insanity of one of the partners, or decree of court.

Party Wall. One wall separating adjoining land owned by different parties used by both estates.

Pass Book. A book furnished by a bank to its depositors in which is shown entries made to the credit of their accounts. It is balanced at intervals to show the debits, or amounts that have been paid out, and the cancelled checks which show these debits are returned (except by savings banks) to the depositor at the time his book is balanced.

Passport. Permits furnished to citizens of the United States to travel unmolested in foreign countries. Can only be issued by the Secretary of State of the United States at Washington and Ministers or other diplomats representing the United States abroad.

Patent. Letters Patent are a grant, issued by the Commissioner of Patents of The United States of America at Washington, D. C., of the exclusive right of an inventor (his heirs or assigns) to make, use and vend his invention throughout the United States and the Territories thereof for a period of seventeen years.

Per Diem. Per day. By the day.

Per Se. By itself, or himself.

Personal Property.	Lares and Penates. Chattels. Property not real estate.
Petty Cash Book.	A book used to keep account of small disbursements, such as towel supply, stamps, soap, etc., etc.
Physical Condition.	(Railroad) Condition of the railroad property, structures and buildings, roadbed, equipments, etc.
Plant	The buildings, machinery, appliances, etc.,

used in the conduct of a manufacturing or other business.

Point.	One per cent.

Postage.

CLASSIFICATION AND RATES OF POSTAGE.

DOMESTIC MAIL MATTER includes mail addressed for local delivery, or for transmission from one place to another within the United States, or to or from or between the possessions of the United States, and to that for transmission to or from the United States or its possessions and officers or members of crews of United States naval vessels, and to or from the United States postal agency at Shanghai, China, and to officers and men of the United States Navy in the United States Naval Hospital at Yokohama, Japan, and is divided into four classes: FIRST, SECOND, THIRD and FOURTH. See *Parcel Post*.

Domestic rates and conditions, with certain exceptions, apply to mail addressed to Canada, Cuba, Mexico, and the Republic of Panama. The domestic rates apply also to letters, but not to other articles, addressed to Great Britain, Ireland, Newfoundland, Bahamas, Barbadoes, British Honduras, Dutch West Indies, Leeward Islands, and to letters for Germany dispatched only by steamers which sail direct to German ports.

PREPAYMENT OF POSTAGE on domestic matter at time of mailing, by stamps affixed, is required. By special permission, however, postage on matter of the third and fourth classes mailed in quantities of not less than 2,000 identical pieces may be paid in money.

CONCEALED MATTER. Matter of a higher class inclosed with matter of a lower class subjects the whole to the higher rate. Persons knowingly concealing or inclosing matter of a higher class in that of a lower class, for the purpose of evading payment of the proper postage, are liable to a fine of not more than $100.

FIRST-CLASS MATTER.

FIRST-CLASS MATTER INCLUDES written matter, namely: Letters, postal cards, post cards (private mailing cards), and all matter wholly or partly in writing, whether sealed or unsealed (except manuscript copy accompanying proof-sheets or corrected proof-sheets of the same and the writing authorized by law on matter of other classes). Also matter sealed or otherwise closed against inspection.

RATES OF POSTAGE. Letters and other first-class matter

two CENTS for each ounce or fraction thereof. Post cards and postal cards ONE CENT each.

"DROP LETTERS," addressed for delivery at the office where mailed, one cent for each ounce or fraction thereof when deposited at post offices where letter carrier service is not established. Letters addressed to patrons served by rural or star route carriers, or deposited in boxes along such routes, are subject to postage at the rate of two cents an ounce or fraction thereof. There is no drop rate on mail other than letters.

THE LIMIT OF WEIGHT of first-class matter is four pounds.

SECOND-CLASS MATTER.

SECOND-CLASS MATTER INCLUDES newspapers and periodicals bearing notice of entry as second-class matter. No limit of weight is prescribed.

RATE OF POSTAGE. Newspapers and periodical publications of the second class, when sent unsealed by others than the publisher or a news agent, ONE CENT FOR EACH FOUR OUNCES, or fraction thereof, on each separately addressed copy or package of unaddressed copies. To be entitled to this rate the copies must be complete. Incomplete copies are third-class matter.

ADDITIONS TO SECOND-CLASS MATTER. On the wrapper, or the matter itself, there may be written or printed: (1) the name and address of the sender, preceded by the word "from"; (2) the name and address of the person to whom sent; (3) the words "sample copy", or "marked copy", or both, as the case may be.

On the matter itself the sender may place all that is permitted on the wrapper; correct typographical errors in the text; designate by marks, not by words, a word or passage in the text to which it is desired to call attention.

Other writing will subject the package to the first-class rate.

Third-Class Matter.

Third-Class Matter Embraces circulars, newspapers and periodicals not admitted to the second-class, nor embraced in the term "book", miscellaneous printed matter on paper not having the nature of an actual personal correspondence, proof-sheets, corrected proof-sheets, and manuscript copy accompanying the same, and matter in point print or raised characters used by the blind. (Books are included in fourth-class or parcel post mail.)

Typewriting and carbon and letter-press copies thereof are the equivalent of hand-writing and are classed as such in all cases. Matter produced by the photographic process (including blue prints), is printed matter. Matter printed on material other than paper is fourth-class.

Circulars. A circular is a printed letter sent in identical terms to several persons. It may bear a written, typewritten, or hand-stamped date, name and address of person addressed and of the sender, and correction of mere typographical errors. When a name (except that of the addressee or sender), date (other than that of the circular), or anything else is handwritten or typewritten in the body of a circular for any other reason than to correct a genuine typographical error, the circular is subject to postage at the first-class (letter) rate, whether sealed or unsealed.

Reproductions or imitations of handwriting and typewriting obtained by means of the printing press, neostyle, multigraph, or similar mechanical process will be treated as third-class matter, provided they are mailed at the post office or other depository designated by the postmaster in a minimum number of 20 identical, unsealed copies. If mailed elsewhere or in less quantity, they will be subject to the first-class rate.

Matter for the Blind. Letters and reading matter for the blind are transmissible in the mails under certain conditions at special rates, which may be ascertained from the postmaster.

THE RATE OF POSTAGE on unsealed third-class matter is ONE CENT FOR EACH TWO OUNCES OR FRACTION THEREOF, on each individually addressed piece or package.

THE LIMIT OF WEIGHT of third-class matter is four pounds. Parcels of printed matter weighing more than four pounds which do not exceed the limit of weight and size for fourth-class matter come within that class and are mailable at the parcel post rates.

ADDITIONS TO THIRD-CLASS MATTER. On the wrapper, envelope, or the tag or label attached thereto, or upon the matter itself, in addition to the name and address of the addressee, there may be written or printed the name, occupation, and residence, or business address, of the sender preceded by the word "from". There may also be placed on the wrapper, envelope, tag, or label, either written or otherwise, the inscription "Do not open until Christmas", or words to that effect, and any printed matter mailable as third-class, but there must be left on the address side a space sufficient for a legible address, postmark and the necessary postage stamps.

The words "Please send out", or "Post up", or other similar directions or requests, not a part of the address, nor necessarily to effect delivery, may not be placed upon the wrapper of third-class matter or upon the matter itself without subjecting it to postage at the letter rate.

On the matter itself the sender may place all that is permitted on the wrapper, and may make marks other than by written or printed words to call attention to any word or passage in the text, and may correct any typographical errors. There may also be written or printed upon any photograph, or other matter of the third-class, a simple manuscript dedication or inscription not in the nature of personal correspondence. Such words as "Dear Sir", "My dear friend", "Yours truly", "Sincerely yours", "Merry Christmas", "Happy New Year", and "With best wishes", written upon third-class matter, are permissible inscriptions. A serial number written or impressed upon third-class matter does not affect its classification.

Written designation of contents, such as "printed matter", "photo", is permissible upon the wrapper of third-class matter.

Inclosures. A single card bearing the written name and address of the sender, or an envelope bearing a written or printed name and address of the sender, may be inclosed with a circular or other third-class matter without affecting its classification.

Hand-stamped imprints on third-class matter will not affect its classification except when the added matter is in itself personal or converts the original matter into a personal communication; in the latter case, however, the mailing at one time at the post office window or other depository designated by the postmaster of not less than 20 identical, unsealed copies will be sufficient evidence of impersonal character to entitle such matter to the third-class rate.

Corrections in proof-sheets include the alteration of the text and insertion of new matter, as well as the correction of typographical and other errors; include also marginal instructions to the printer necessary to the correction of the matter or its proper appearance in print. Part of an article may be entirely rewritten if that be necessary for correction. Corrections should be upon the margin of or attached to the proof-sheets. Manuscript of one article cannot be inclosed with proof or corrected proof-sheets of another except at the first-class rate.

Fourth-Class Matter.
See *Parcel Post*.

Because of carelessness in addressing and preparing matter for mailing, or failure of sender to place his or her name and address on it, millions of letters and other pieces of mail which cannot be delivered or returned to sender, are each year sent to the Division of Dead Letters. The practice of some business concerns of omitting street numbers, etc., from their stationery and advertisements results in increasing the volume of insufficiently addressed mail.

```
After — days return to
    JOHN C. SMITH,                          Stamp.
    146 State St.,
  Wilkesville, N. Y.



            MR.  FRANK B.  JONES,
               2416 Front Street,
                    OSWEGO,
                             OHIO.
```

```
After — days return to
    JOHN C. SMITH,                          Stamp.
  Rural Route No. 1,
  Wilkesville, N. Y.



            MR.  FRANK B.  JONES,
              Rural Route No.  3,
                    OSWEGO,
                             OHIO.
```

MODEL FORMS OF ADDRESSES.

Write plainly the name of the person addressed, street and number, or number of rural route, post office and state in full. When the name of the state is abbreviated, frequently Va. and Pa., Md. and Ind., Colo. and Cal., Miss. and Minn., and others are confused and mail missent, as post offices of the same name are located in several states. See *Abbreviations*.

Do not abbreviate or use lead pencil.

Unmailable domestic matter includes: address defective, postage not prepaid, overweight and oversize, game killed or offered in violation of law, meat and meat-food products, nursery stock without required certificate of inspection or exemption; poisons, liquors, live animals, fowls, etc.; tinsel and glass (unless properly wrapped or enclosed); obscene and indecent matter; defamatory, dunning, etc.; lottery and fraud.

Postage stamps are sold in denominations of 1, 2, 3, 4, 5, 6, 7, 8, 9, 10, 12, 15, 20, 30 and 50-cent; 1, 2 and 5-dollar; and 10-cent special delivery.

When stamps are affixed to mail so that one overlies another concealing part of its surface, the stamp thus covered is not taken into account in prepayment.

GENERAL DELIVERY. The general delivery is intended for the use of only those patrons who are not permanently located or who cannot, for good and sufficient reasons, receive mail by carrier or through a post office box. The general delivery should not be used where it is possible to receive mail otherwise. Persons intending to remain for thirty days or more in a city having carrier service should file their names and street address at the post office so that their mail may be delivered by carrier.

Persons applying for mail at the general delivery window, if unknown, may be required to prove their identity, and residents of cities having carrier service who call at the general delivery may be required to furnish a statement as to name and address and reason for calling at post office for mail instead of receiving it by carrier.

POST OFFICE BOXES are provided for the convenience of the public in the delivery of mail. Box rents must be paid quarterly in advance. The use of a box is restricted to one individual, family, firm, or corporation.

The renter of a box may have delivered through it mail for his family, guests, transient boarders, employees who are members of his household, and, for a period not to exceed thirty days, mail of a person addressed in his care.

A box rented by a firm may be used for the delivery of its mail, and by the consent of each member of the firm, the individual mail of each, of his household, and of the firm's office employees.

A box rented by a corporation, association, or society may be used for the delivery of mail addressed to it and its officials.

Boxes rented by schools, colleges, or public institutions, if consistent with the rules and usage thereof, may be used for the delivery of mail addressed to officers, students, employees and inmates.

HUSBAND OR WIFE. Neither husband nor wife can control the delivery of mail addressed to the other against the wishes of the one to whom it is addressed. In the absence of instructions to the contrary, the wife's letters will be placed in the husband's box and delivered to him with his letters, unless they be known to live separately.

WRONG DELIVERY. A person receiving mail not intended for him should return it promptly to the post office for proper disposition. If such mail has been opened by mistake it should be endorsed, ''Opened by mistake'', with the signature of the person receiving it.

SPECIAL DELIVERY SERVICE is the prompt delivery of

mail by messenger during prescribed hours to persons who reside within the carrier limits of city delivery offices, to patrons of rural service who reside more than one mile from post offices but within one-half mile of rural routes, and to residents within one mile of any post office. Special delivery mail is not expedited in transit between post offices.

RECALL OF MAIL. When the sender of a letter desires to recall it, his application must be submitted to the postmaster at the office of mailing.

UNDELIVERABLE LETTERS AND SEALED PARCELS (FIRST-CLASS MATTER), which cannot be delivered to addressees or returned to senders, are sent to the Division of Dead Letters for disposal. Such matter includes unclaimed, misdirected, unaddressed and insufficiently prepaid letters and those directed to initials only or to fictitious persons. Letters are opened and returned to writers, if practicable, except such as contain advertising matter only, the return of which is not requested. If valuable inclosures are found, a record is made, and if not returned at once to the owner, they may be reclaimed within four years from the date of their receipt.

UNDELIVERABLE PARCELS OF THIRD AND FOURTH-CLASS MATTER of obvious value which cannot be returned to the sender, and articles found loose in the mails, except money and postage stamps, are sent to the post office at the headquarters of the division of the Railway Mail Service in which the parcels or articles are detained, where they are held for twelve months, subject to inquiry, after which they cannot be reclaimed.   Matter addressed to foreign countries mailed in violation of law or treaty stipulation is sent to the Division of Dead Letters.

APPROXIMATE TIME OF MAILS FROM NEW YORK

This table shows the transit time (approximately by through trains) of letter mails despatched from the New York Post Office.   About two or three hours additional should be allowed for handling the mails and conveying them between post offices and railroad stations.

Name of Place	Hours	Name of Place	Hours
ALABAMA		**LOUISIANA**	
Birmingham	32	New Orleans	41
Montgomery	32	Shreveport	46
ARIZONA		**MAINE**	
Phoenix	76	Augusta	15
Prescott	83	Portland	11
ARKANSAS		**MARYLAND**	
Hot Springs	37	Baltimore	5
Little Rock	33	**MASSACHUSETTS**	
CALIFORNIA		Boston	6
Fresno	92	Lowell	8
Los Angeles	92	Springfield	4
Pasadena	92	Worcester	5
Sacramento	82	**MICHIGAN**	
San Diego	102	Detroit	16
San Francisco	85	Grand Rapids	21
San Jose	87	**MINNESOTA**	
COLORADO		Duluth	40
Colorado Springs	57	Minneapolis	35
Denver	52	St. Paul	34
CONNECTICUT		**MISSISSIPPI**	
Bridgeport	1½	Greenville	45
Hartford	3½	Jackson	39
New Haven	2	Meridian	36
Stamford	1½	Vicksburg	44
FLORIDA		**MISSOURI**	
Jacksonville	29	Kansas City	32
Key West	48	St. Joseph	33
Miami	43	St. Louis	25
Tallahassee	32	**MONTANA**	
GEORGIA		Butte	70
Atlanta	26	Helena	66
Columbus	32	**NEBRASKA**	
Savannah	30	Omaha	35
IDAHO		**NEVADA**	
Boise City	70	Carson City	84
ILLINOIS		Reno	74
Chicago	24	**NEW HAMPSHIRE**	
Danville	29	Concord	9½
Peoria	28	**NEW JERSEY**	
Rockford	28	Atlantic City	5
Springfield	30	Trenton	1½
INDIANA		**NEW MEXICO**	
Indianapolis	19	Albuquerque	57
IOWA		**NEW YORK**	
Des Moines	35	Albany	3½
Sioux City	42	Binghamton	6
KANSAS		Buffalo	11
Kansas City	32	Elmira	8
Topeka	34	Rochester	9
KENTUCKY		Syracuse	7
Frankfort	31	Troy	4
Louisville	24	Utica	5½
		Watertown	10

Photograph by G. V. Buck, Washington, D. C. From Underwood & Underwood, N. Y.

THE ANNUAL DEAD LETTER SALE OF THE POST OFFICE DEPARTMENT

Name of Place	Hours	Name of Place	Hours
NORTH CAROLINA		Memphis	31
Charlotte	18	Nashville	27
Raleigh	19	TEXAS	
Wilmington	21	Dallas	49
NORTH DAKOTA		El Paso	65
Bismark	50	Galveston	53
Grand Forks	47	Houston	49
OHIO		San Antonio	60
Cincinnati	17	UTAH	
Cleveland	14	Ogden	62
Columbus	14	Salt Lake City	63
Dayton	26	VERMONT	
Springfield	21	Burlington	7
Toledo	18	Montpelier	11
Youngstown	12	VIRGINIA	
PENNSYLVANIA		Richmond	11
Erie	12	WASHINGTON	
Harrisburg	5	Seattle	81
Philadelphia	2½	Spokane	69
Pittsburgh	11	Tacoma	82
Reading	5	WEST VIRGINIA	
Scranton	4	Wheeling	14
Wilkes-Barre	6	WISCONSIN	
Williamsport	8	Milwaukee	27
RHODE ISLAND		WYOMING	
Providence	5	Cheyenne	43
SOUTH CAROLINA		CANADA	
Charleston	26	Calgary	75
Columbia	20	Halifax	34
SOUTH DAKOTA		Montreal	12
Aberdeen	48	Quebec	20
TENNESSEE		Toronto	16
Chattanooga	25	Vancouver	97
		Winnipeg	50

MAIL TIME AND DISTANCES

New York to European Points

Places and Countries.	Miles.	Days.	Places and Countries.	Miles.	Days.
Alexandria, Egypt	6,150	13	Hamburg, Germany	4,820	9
Algiers, Algeria	5,030	10	Havre, France	3,940	8
Amsterdam, Holland	3,985	9	Lisbon, Portugal	5,335	10
Antwerp, Belgium	4,000	9	Liverpool, England	3,540	8
Athens, Greece	5,655	12	London, England	3,740	8
Basel, Switzerland	4,420	9	Lucerne, Switzerland	4,480	9
Barcelona, Spain	4,790	10	Lyons, France	4,340	9
Berlin, Germany	4,385	9	Madrid, Spain	4,925	10
Berne, Switzerland	4,490	9	Milan, Italy	4,615	9
Bordeaux, France	4,388	9	Moscow, Russia	5,535	10
Bremen, Germany	4,235	8	Munich, Bavaria	4,610	9
Brussels, Belgium	3,975	9	Naples, Italy	5,195	9
Cadiz, Spain	5,375	10	Nice, France	4,700	9
Cairo, Egypt	6,280	12	Odessa, Russia	5,455	11
Christiania, Norway	4,650	10	Paris, France	4,020	8
Cologne, Germany	4,115	8	Queenstown, Ireland	3,250	7
Constantinople, Turkey	5,810	11	Rome, Italy	5,030	9
Copenhagen, Denmark	4,575	10	Rotterdam, Holland	3,935	9
Dresden, Germany	4,555	9	St. Petersburg, Russia	5,370	10
Florence, Italy	4,800	10	Southampton, England	3,680	8
Geneva, Switzerland	4,410	9	Stockholm, Sweden	4,975	10
Genoa, Italy	4,615	9	Venice, Italy	4,780	9
Glasgow, Scotland	3,375	8	Vienna, Austria	4,740	10
Hague, The, Holland	3,950	9	Zurich, Switzerland	4,170	9

Postal Savings. Established for the purpose of providing facilities for depositing savings at interest, with the security of the United States Government for repayment.

An account may be opened by any person 10 years or over in his or her own name, or by a married woman in her own name and free from any control or interference of her husband.

Deposits accepted only from individuals, not in the name of any corporation, association, society, firm or partnership, or in the name of two or more persons jointly, nor in the name of one person in trust for another.

An account may be opened at any depository post office, but no person may have more than one postal savings account at the same office or at different offices.

All accounts shall be opened by the depositor in person or his authorized representative. After opening the account, the depositor may send future deposits by registered mail or money order made payable to the postmaster.

No account may be opened for less than $1., nor will fractions of a dollar be accepted for deposit. No person is permitted to deposit more than $100. in any one calendar month nor to have a total balance to his credit at any one time of more than $500. exclusive of accumulated interest.

Amounts less than $1 may be saved for deposit by purchasing 10-cent postal saving cards and 10 cent postal saving stamps.

Interest at the rate of 2% per annum is allowed on the amount represented by each postal savings certificate, payable annually. Interest will not be paid for a fraction of a year. Interest will continue to accrue annually on a postal savings certificate as long as it remains outstanding, certificates being valid until paid, without limitation as to time. Compound interest is not allowed on an outstanding certificate, but a depositor may withdraw interest accrued and make a new deposit, subject to the restriction that deposits at interest will not be received for less than $1.

Certificates are not transferable or negotiable.

A depositor may exchange the whole or any part of his deposits in sums of $20, or any multiple of $20 up to and including $500, for United States registered or coupon bonds bearing interest at the rate of 2½% per annum, payable semi-annually, redeemable at the pleasure of the United States after one year from date of issue, and both principal and interest being payable 20 years from such date in United States gold coin. The exchange may be made as of January 1 and July 1 of each year.

Pound.   See *Coins*.

Power of Attorney.   An instrument, duly signed and witnessed, wherein one person confers upon another the authority to act in his name and stead. The power may be general—to transact all business —or special—the particular matter cited in the P. A.

FORM OF POWER OF ATTORNEY.

🕮 Know all Men by these Presents,

That ....

have made, constituted and appointed, and by these presents do........

make, constitute and appoint...................................
......true and lawful attorney.........for............and in........
name, place and stead...
giving and granting unto..........said attorney....full power and au-
thority to do and perform all and every act and thing whatsoever requi-
site and necessary to be done in and about the premises as fully to all
intents and purposes as................might or could do if personally
present, with full power of substitution and revocation, hereby verifying
and confirming all that..........said attorney........or............
substitute shall lawfully do or cause to be done by virtue hereof.

In Witness whereof, *have hereunto set........hand......and seal*
the.................day of...................in the year nineteen
hundred and..

Sealed and Delivered in the presence of

Forms of signature of an agent acting under a Power of Attorney.

JOHN SMITH & Co..
per pro Walter Girard

or

PER PRO JOHN SMITH & Co.,
Walter Girard.

or

p.p. JOHN SMITH & Co.,
Walter Girard.

Preferred Stock. See *Bonds and Stocks.*

Premium. (Insurance) The rate paid periodically for insurance.

Any amount paid in consideration of money loaned. An excess amount. A bonus. A gratuitous sum paid as an incentive.

(Finance) The amount paid over and above the face or par value of a stock or bond; e. g., a share originally issued at a par value of $100 and sold at $110 is said to be sold at a PREMIUM of 10%. In this connection it is also used to mean of exceptional value and hence not easy to obtain. See *Discount.*

Present Standard of Weight and Fineness. See *Standard of Weight and Fineness.*

Prima Facie. At first sight.

Principal. The major part, as the PRINCIPAL of an estate; the corpus. Superior. Chief. (Finance) The amount from which income is derived.

Principle. Doctrine; rule; motive; element; rudiment; source. Ex. The fundamental PRINCIPLES of International Law.

Prior Lien A valid claim which takes precedence over all others. First lien.

Produce Exchange. The New York Produce Exchange is located corner of Beaver Street and Broadway. It was established in 1862, has over 2,000 members and deals in grains, cotton-seed oil and other provisions, but principally in wheat. It was also authorized by legislature, in 1907, to deal in securities.

Promissory See *Notes.*
Note.

Promoter A person engaged in the business of organ-
izing and securing capital to operate a new
company, or to augment the capital of a going concern.

Proof of Loss. A statement in the form of an affidavit de-
scribing property or document lost. See
Care of Important Papers.

FORM OF STATEMENT AND PROOF OF LOSS.

For Claims Less than $100

To the .... **INSURANCE COMPANY.**
The property described in your Policy No.............of..........
Agency, insuring ....
issued for the term of..............from ....19....to
.....................19....was damaged by a fire which occurred
on the ....day of ....19......
caused by ....
The ownership and location of said property are as stated in said
Policy; and the cash value thereof, the whole insurance and loss thereon, together with the insurance by and the claim upon you, are as
follows :—

DESCRIPTION OF PROPERTY	CASH VALUE	WHOLE INSURANCE	WHOLE LOSS	INSURANCE BY ABOVE CO.	CLAIM UPON ABOVE CO.

There was .... incumbrance upon said property; and besides your Policy there was only.........................Dollars
other insurance, all of which covered in like manner.
The buildings referred to in said Policy were occupied only as
permitted therein; and the said fire did not originate by any act, design
or procurement, on the part of the insured, or prohibited by said Policy;

and nothing has been done before or since the fire by said insured, or by the party making this statement and proof, to violate any of the conditions of said policy.

In accordance with the foregoing........claim.................... Dollars, as your share of the loss.

....Claimant.

Subscribed and sworn to before me, this....................day of ....19....

....

I hereby certify that the foregoing claim is just and true.

....Agent.

$....................

Receíveð at.................... on the ....day of ....19....of the.................... **INSURANCE COMPANY** of ....Dollars, in full satisfaction of all claims for loss and damage by fire as stated above, under Policy No. .... of ....Agency, and in consideration thereof ....hereby release and discharge the said Company from all claims whatsoever growing out of said fire loss or damage, directly or indirectly, and the amount of said Policy is hereby reduced in the above-mentioned sum, leaving the sum of....................Dollars only in force on said Policy.   Witness my hand and seal,

....(L. s.)

Statement and Proof of Loss

For Claims less than $100.

No..........

N. Y. Board of Fire Underwriters' Form

Assured

Policy No....

Agency.

Amount of Policy, $....................

Amount of Claim, $....................

Amount Paid, $....................

Date of Fire....

Proofs Received ....

Date of Payment....................

Adjuster.

Insurance Co.

of

Schedule of Total Insurance and Apportionment of Claim

COMPANY	AM'T INSURED	AM'T CLAIMED	COMPANY	AM'T INSURED	AM'T CLAIMED

DUPLICATE RECEIPT

$.....................

Received at ....on the...............
day of.............................19....of the.................
.... **INSURANCE COMPANY**
of...Dollars, in full
satisfaction of all claims for loss and damage by fire as stated above,
under Policy No.................of......................Agency,
and in consideration thereof.........hereby release and discharge the
said Company from all claims whatsoever growing out of said fire loss
or damage, directly or indirectly, and the amount of said Policy is
hereby reduced in the above-mentioned sum, leaving the sum of......
....Dollars only in force on said
Policy. Witness my hand and seal.

....[L. S.]

Proof. GALLEY PROOF—The first proof, taken on long narrow sheets without regard to paging, which has been printed from type set in a Galley— an oblong, brass or metal tray used to hold type.

PRINTER'S PROOF—Corrections in printers' proofs should be made in red ink in the margin, never with pencil.

The following symbols are commonly used in correcting proof:

· PROOF MARKS ·

MARGINAL MARK	CORRESPONDING MARK IN PROOF	MEANING
of	He made his mar*f*k	*take out*
⊂⊃	He ma⊃de his mark	*close up*
⑨	He m⑨de his mark	*invert*
∟	∟ He made his mark	*bring to mark*
tr	He his made mark	*transpose*
stet	He made his mark	*let stand*
(t.?)	He made his mark	*query to author*
¶	·Therefore, be it Resolved	*make paragraph*
☐	He made his mark	*indent em-quad*
wr.f.	He made his mark	*wrong font letter*
l. c.	He made his Mark	*lower case letter*
sm. c.	He made his mark	*small capital*
caps	He made his mark	*capitals*
italic	He made his mark	*put in italic*
roman	He made *bis* mark	*put in roman*
○	He made his mark	*period*
˅	He made Johns mark	*apostrophe*
˅ ˅	He made his mark	*quotation marks*
-/	This is a trademark	*hyphen*
#	He made hismark	*space*
˅ ⋀	He made his mark	*even spacing*
⊥	He made his mark	*push down space*
✕	He made his mark	*broken letter*

THE above marks are the ones most generally used in proofreading. There are many others that are required in different classes of work, but these are in the main self-explanatory. This display of proof marks and their meanings has been prepared for THE GRAPHIC ARTS and endorsed by the Boston Proofreaders Association.

THE GRAPHIC ARTS, BOSTON

See *Type.*

Prospectus. A descriptive booklet or circular, distributed for the purpose of making known the salient and attractive features of an enterprise.

Pro Tem. (Tempore). For the time being. Ex: President PRO TEM.

Protest. The declaration of a Notary Public that a note or check has been presented and payment refused. See *Notes* and *Checks*.

Proxy. An agent, or one who is authorized to vote or act for another. The paper itself, viz:

FORM OF PROXY.

Know all Men by these Presents, *That I,* ....
do hereby constitute and appoint....................................
Attorney......and Agent......for me, and in my name, place and stead,
to vote as my proxy at...............of the........................
according to the number of *votes that I should be entitled to vote, if*
then personally present.

In Witness Whereof, *I have hereunto set my hand and seal this*
................day of...............one thousand nine hundred and

Sealed and Delivered in the Presence of

Public Utilities. Public Utility or Public Service securities are stocks and bonds of corporations serving the general public, i. e., street railway, gas, electric light, water companies, etc.

Punctuation.

PUNCTUATION MARKS, ETC.

Period	.	Caret	∧
Interrogation-point .	?	Dieresis	ö
Exclamation-point .	!	Asterisk	*
Colon	:	Daggers	† or ‡
Semicolon	;	Paragraph	¶
Comma	,	Section	§
Quotation-marks . .	" " or ' '	Breve	ă
Apostrophe . . .	'	Macron	ā
Dash	—	Ditto	"
Hyphen	-	Cedilla	ç
Parenthesis . . .	( )	Tilde	ñ
Brackets . . .	[ ]	Leaders	....
Brace or Bracket .	}	Ellipsis . . .... or —— or * * *	

Should follow:

(1)   A complete declarative or imperative sentence.

> *Examples*:   It snows.
> Do it now.

(2)   Abbreviations.

> *Examples*:   Nov.   inst.   corp.   Dr.   Géo.

Nicknames are not abbreviations and should not be followed by a period: as, *Al Tom Ben*

The period after the abbreviation is independent of other punctuation in the sentence. *"I myself brought the letter to the P. O.; there is no doubt of that."*

When an abbreviated word ends a sentence, only one period is necessary. *They delivered the cargo on the* 30*th inst.*

Contractions should not be followed by a period *Ass'n Rec'd Dep't*

(3)   The unit, separating it from the decimal.

> *Examples*:   5.05% $109.50.

When periods are used to show the omission of letters, one dot should be used for each letter omitted: *Secretary L.....g. (Lansing).*

Periods are used to carry the eye from words at the beginning of a line to matter at its end.   They are called leaders, and are used in billing, in the index of a book, the contents, etc.

INTERROGATION-POINT

Should follow:

(1) Every *direct* question.

> *Examples:*
> (Direct) When will you return?
> (Indirect) She asked me when I would return.

(2) Interrogative clause or clauses interjected into an affirmative sentence.

> *Example:* The questions now raised, How shall we feed our unemployed? Where house them? require an immediate answer.

(3) Elliptical questions of common dependence.

> *Example:* What is meant by "hypothecate"? by "arbitage"? by "inalienable right"? and by "margin of profit"?

(4) An assertion that is subject to doubt.

> *Example:* She claims she can typewrite 149 words a minute (?) from new matter.

Sometimes a statement declarative in form is in reality interrogative and takes a question-mark after it; as "You will stay with her to the end?"

EXCLAMATION-POINT

Should follow:

(1) Interjections.

> *Examples:* Alas! Oh! Ah! Hold! Gracious!

(2) Exclamatory phrases and sentences.

> *Examples*: (Phrases) How lovely! We make over a machine a minute—just think!
>
> (Sentences) How suggestive of the South are those magnolias! How quickly Time flies! Oh, wouldn't it be exciting to be shipwrecked!

More than one exclamation-point is used to indicate an extraordinary degree of emotion, or for emphasis.

> *Examples*: "A Perfect Woman!! Where can such a creature be found?"
>
> This stock must be sold below cost!!!

COLON

Should follow:

(1) The salutation of a business letter.

> Dear Sir: Dear Madam: My dear Sir:

(2) Words introducing an array of particulars that are separated by commas or semicolons.

> *Examples*: The business woman has two uniforms: either a one-piece cloth dress with smart collars and cuffs, or a simple shirt waist and skirt.
>
> She had all the qualities of a successful business woman: tact, loyalty, thoughtfulness, courtesy, ability.
>
> "My reasons for not employing her were three: first, she was too glib in her speech, agreeing with what was said before it was said, showing a certain flippancy in thought; second, her speech was largely slang, which indicated lack of refinement; third, her style of dress was so extreme as to be conspicuous."—(*Good Housekeeping Magazine*.)

(3) Words such as *thus, this, as follows, these, following, to wit.*

(4) Words introducing a direct quotation.

> *Example*: Her telegram reads: "Find my train does not reach New York until three-thirty."

Should separate:

(1) Clauses that are but slightly connected. (In almost every case, however, a new sentence would be preferable.)

> *Example*: As in all other professions, there is an ever-increasing demand for the highly expert: those who are thoroughly capable need not fear lack of employment.

(2) Clauses grammatically complete in themselves, not connected by a conjunction, but depending upon each other to convey the full force of the remark.

> *Example*: You can lead a horse to water: you cannot make him drink.

(3) Members of a compound sentence the minor divisions of which are separated by semicolons.

> *Example*: "We never, in a moral way, applaud or blame either ourselves or others for what we enjoy or suffer; or for having impressions made upon us which we consider as being altogether out of our power: but only for what we do, or would have done had it been in our power; or for what we leave undone which we might have done, or would have left undone though we could have done it."—*Bishop Butler.*

(4) Numerals denoting time.

> *Examples*: 5:30 p.m. Will return on the 8:05.

The colon is used to separate parts of a sentence that are not so closely connected as to warrant a semicolon, yet closely enough connected as not to require the full stop.

Semicolon

Should be placed:

(1) Between closely connected clauses of a compound sentence when no conjunction is used.

> *Examples*: We take care of our health; we lay up money; we make our roof tight and our clothing sufficient; but who provides wisely that he shall not be wanting in the best property of all—friends?—*Emerson*.

In sentences like the following where the clauses are short, commas may be used.

> She has her business; she has her profession; she has her office.

(2) Before the conjunctions *for, therefore, hence,* and usually *but*.

> *Examples*: The telephone company, it is said, loses 125 hours a day through the use of the word "please" by its operators; hence courtesy would seem an item of great expense to them.
>
> Many stenographers can use the typewriter and write shorthand; but grammar and spelling are unknown to them.

(3) Before the conjunction *as* when it introduces **an** example.

> *Example*: *Per* should be affixed only to words of Latin origin; as, per diem, per cent., per annum, per capita, per se.

(4) Between the members of a compound sentence, the minor divisions of which are separated by commas.

> *Example*: Be done with saying what you don't believe, and find somewhere or other, the truest, divinest thing to your soul, that you do believe to-day, and work that out; work it out with all the action and consecration of your soul, in the doing of your work.—*Phillips Brooks*.

Should separate:

A series of clauses beginning with the word *that*.

> *Example*: "It is rather for us to be here dedicated to the great task remaining before us; that from these honored dead we take increased devotion to that cause for which they gave the last full measure of devotion; that we here highly resolve that these dead shall not have died in vain; that this nation, under God, shall have a new birth of freedom, and that government of the people by the people and for the people shall not perish from the earth."

The semicolon is used to separate parts of a sentence more closely connected than to require a colon, yet not so closely connected as to require a comma.

Comma

Rules for the use of the comma are difficult to apply in commercial correspondence; it is largely a matter of individual taste. One may err on the side of too many commas, or not enough; although it is better to have too few than too many. The following rules, however, are generally adhered to:

A comma is used:

(1) To separate a series of words (singly or in pairs), phrases, or short clauses.

When a series of words *with no conjunction between them* form the subject of a sentence, a comma separates the last word from the predicate.

> *Example*: Regularity, punctuality, personality, are her chief assets.

When a series of words *with* a conjunction between the last two form the subject of the sentence, the comma is placed before the coniunction to show that the last two are no more closely connected in the construction than the preceding words of the series.

> *Example*: Regularity, punctuality, personality, dignity, ability, and sociability are the office girl's assets.

When the subject consists of a series of words *connected by a conjunction,* no comma separates it from the predicate. (See example last above given.)

> IN PAIRS—A small *f* and *t*, a capital *L* and hyphen, a capital *L* and period; these all may be used to indicate the pound Sterling mark.
>
> PHRASES—Ability to spell, to punctuate properly, to be grammatically accurate, to have a talent for clear, logical expression, lifts the stenographer into the secretary class.
>
> CLAUSES—Your hands are not properly cared for, your hair is coming down, your petticoat shows under your skirt, and altogether you seem to be entirely indifferent to your personal appearance.

(2) Between words where a conjunction or a verb previously used is omitted.

> *Examples*: Neither envy, jealousy, hatred, nor revenge will make for happiness. (*nor* is omitted after *envy* and *jealousy*.)
>
> I will work hard, conscientiously, systematically, and cheerfully to bring about the result you wish. (*and* is omitted after *hard* and *conscientiously*.)
>
> A competency is desired by many; riches, by few. (*is desired* is omitted after *riches*.)

(3) To enclose parenthetical, explanatory, independent, or synonymous expressions.

> *Examples*:
> On the whole
> It seems to me
> She said
> Per se
> Too (except when it occurs at the end of a line. "I shall be there too.")

Investment funds, or capital, will be hard to obtain.

I turned and saw a young woman, rather tawdrily dressed, coming toward me.

If the explanatory expression is necessary to the sense of the *whole* sentence (restrictive) no comma is needed.

Examples: Did you see the typist dressed in brown?

Did you see the typist, who is dressed in brown?

(4) To separate words in apposition from the remainder of the sentence. (Exception, when but one word is used in apposition.)

Examples: Miss Alberts, one of the cleverest politicians in the country, then addressed the meeting.

My sister Margaret will be here shortly.

(5) To separate from the rest of the sentence transpositions, or clauses placed out of their natural order, as when a dependent clause is placed before the principal clause.

Examples: Try as I will, I cannot distinguish between shall and will.

In my presence, you may not speak of my friend so.

(6) Between the members of a compound sentence connected by *and, but, or, for, because, whereas,*

and other conjunctions, when the meaning is but *slightly* changed. (A decided change in meaning or thought calls for a semicolon.)

Examples: She has her office, but she wants a home.

Write out AND in the names of railroads, but use the sign & in the names of firms.

The keys of the typewriter are arranged with reference to the frequency with which the letters are used, and the order in which they commonly occur.

We lie abed when we are sick, but get up when we are well.

We lay a thing down, in order to set it in its place.

(7) To separate the name of a person directly addressed from the rest of the sentence.

Example: "Take this letter, Miss Smith, and make a copy of it."

(8) To separate introductory words from a direct quotation, when both are short.

Example: The telegram reads, "Arrive on the five-thirty." (If either the quotation or the introductory sentence is long, they are separated by a colon.)

(9) To cut off contrasting (antithetical) expressions.

Examples: She is as tall, though not so handsome, as her sister.

Contentment consists not in great wealth, but in few wants.—*Epicurus*.

(10) Between words repeated.

Examples: Many, many times, have I seen it turn out as you say.

When I return the report to you, you will see what I mean. (Better construction would be: You will see my meaning when I return the report to you.)

No comma is placed, however, between words repeated in such expressions as: "We have come to dedicate a portion of that field as a final resting place for those who here gave their lives that that nation might live."

(11) To point off figures.

Example: $9,999,999,999.

(12) At the end of each line of the address and complimentary close of a letter.

Examples: Mr. George Carey,
West New Brighton, S. I.,
New York.

With best regards,
Sincerely yours,

I am, dear sir,
Yours very truly,

I remain,
Very truly yours,

(13) Before *to* when equivalent to *in order to*.

Examples: The people of the city, to show their appreciation, elected her Commissioner.

She was sent to France, to complete her education.

(14) To separate a long subject from its verb.

> *Example*: To end a sentence with an adverb or a preposition, weakens it.

QUOTATION-MARKS

(1) Every *direct* quotation should be enclosed in quotation-marks.

> *Examples*: (Direct) "If I employ a secretary," he said frankly, "I want her to look like a business woman."
>
> (Indirect) He told her frankly that if he employed a secretary he wanted her to look like a business woman.

(2) A quotation within a quotation is enclosed with single marks.

> *Example*: Her employer answered: "You would better keep this motto, 'Do It Now' before you."

If there is another quotation within the single marks, double marks are used.

> *Example*: The letter begins: "Dear Madam: Your inquiry, 'Where can I obtain a copy of "The Efficient Secretary" or similar publication,' has been referred to me for reply."

(3) Names of steamers and boats are enclosed in quotation-marks when they are not set in caps or underscored.

> *Examples*: She sailed on the SS. "George Washington" on Decoration Day.
>
> The "Mary Lee," a large tug, appeared alongside.

(4)   Titles of books, plays, works of art, are either set in quotation-marks, underscored, or set in caps.

> *Examples* : Can't you read "East Lynn" sometime this week?
>
> I have heard that "The Girl of the Golden West" is playing in Chicago.
>
> The best statue I saw was "The Thinker" and you will agree with me that it is exquisite.

(5)   When the quotation comprises several successive paragraphs, the marks are placed at the commencement of each paragraph, but at the end of the last paragraph only.

> *Example* :
>
> "I hold it true that thoughts are things
> Endowed with bodies, breath and wings:
> And that we send them forth to fill
> The world with good results—or ill.
>
> "That which we call our secret thought
> Speeds to the earth's remotest spot,
> And leaves its blessings or its woes,
> Like tracks behind it, where it goes.
>
> "It is God's law. Remember it
> In your still chamber as you sit
> With thoughts you would not dare have known
> And yet made comrades when alone.
>
> "These thoughts have life; and they will fly
> And leave their impress by and by,
> Like some marsh breeze whose poisoned breath
> Breathes into homes like fevered death.

"And after you have quite forgot
Or all outgrown some vanished thought,
Back to your mind to make its home,
A dove or raven it will come.

"Then let your secret thoughts be fair;
They have a vital part and share
In shaping worlds and molding fate—
God's system is so intricate."

—*Ella Wheeler Wilcox.*

(6) The quotation-marks are sometimes placed at the beginning of each line and at the end of the quotation.

Example:
"I will be more honest, square, and prompt
"than business requires; more kind than
"charity requires; more loyal than friend-
"ship requires; more thoughtful than love
"requires. I will enjoy as heartily as I
"can what the day brings me; and get
"all the pleasure possible out of eating,
"drinking, working, resting, amusements,
"and the people I meet; so that at night
"I may be able to say: 'I have lived today,
"and have found life good.' "—*Dr. Frank Crane in the New York Globe.*

(7) Expressions introduced by *so-called, self-styled, known as,* and the like, are enclosed in quotation-marks.

Examples: The so-called "Cotton King."
The land known as the "Railroad Reservation."
The self-styled "World's Greatest Magician"

(8) When particular emphasis is to be denoted, or attention called to a word, or when a word is used out of its ordinary meaning, it is enclosed in quotation-marks.

> *Examples*: Your "Personal" favor 23rd instant.
>
> I may gain the respect even of the man who knew me as a child, and that is "some" respect.

(9) The comma and period are almost invariably enclosed within the quotation marks.

> *Example*: "I will make my enforced intimacies as pleasant as possible."

The colon and semicolon may either precede or follow the quotation-mark.

> *Examples*: They had been at the pains to erect "fair and stately houses, wherein they at first outdid the rest of the country"; and they soon found their town become a sort of capital for that part of the shore.
>
> It was he who "preached the funeral sermons to the king, after sentence, out of Esaias": "Thou art cast out of the grave like an abominable branch."

The exclamation-mark and the question-mark are placed within the quotation-marks only when they properly belong to the quoted matter.

Examples: He exclaimed, "How beautifully she sings!"

How strange you have not read Dr. Walton's "Peg Along"!

"Do you use the Touch system?" she asked. Did she ask, "Do you like the Touch system"?

(10) When a quotation is not completed *etc.* or *&c.* should be enclosed within the quotation-marks; or if a *dash* is used to show the ellipsis, it should be within the quotation-marks.

Examples: "No wonder it was a railroad man to whom came the happy thought of dividing the country into time zones, etc."

"—— and smile at mortals who would look beyond."

APOSTROPHE

Is used:

(1) To indicate the possessive case.

Examples: A man's man. Men's shoes. Peck & Smith's store. Sister-in-law's. Everybody else's.

When the singular ends in a sibilant (the sound of S or Z), to form the plural possessive, the apostrophe only is added: *Conscience' sake, Felix' invention, Moses' staff.*

Some authorities say that words of *one* syllable ending in a sibilant take apostrophe *AND S;* as *fox's tracks.*

When the plural ends in S, the apostrophe only is

added: *Kings' daughters, John Brown & Sons' address, Three days' grace.*

Personal pronouns in the possessive case of course do not take an apostrophe: *Mine, Yours, Theirs, His, Hers, Its.*

(2)   To indicate the omission of letters or figures.

Examples:

I'll	I will
e'en	even
don't	do not
let's	let us
o'clock	of the clock
thro'	through
'kerchief	handkerchief
'07	1907
It's	It is (Possessive—Its)
You're	You are (Possessive—Your)
They're	They are (Possessive—Their)

It's immaterial which way you do it.
Its usefulness is over.
You're in the right.
Your gloves are here.
They're good friends.
Their letter of the 1st.

In dialect, to show the omission of letters:

"Dat baby of you's" said Mrs. Jacksing, "am de puffet image ob his fathah."

"Yas," answered Mrs. Johnsing, "He am a reg'lar cahbon copy."—*Remington Notes.*

(3)   To indicate the plural of a letter, word, or figure.

Examples:
Two r's.
"If's and And's."
Baltimore and Ohio 4's (or 4s).

DASH

Is used:

(1) To indicate a pause, faltering, break, or sudden change in thought.

> *Examples*: The world moves but one way—forward.
>
> Evenings at home may be spent profitably if——
>
> This, we maintain, is false economy—plus laziness.
>
> I——I am sorry.
>
> Juli——a!

(2) To indicate the omission of the word *to*.

> *Examples*: May—November; June—December; 1890—1900.

(3) To indicate the omission of a name or date.

> *Examples*: Miss B————
> In the year 19——
> In the town of ————

(4) To cut off words or phrases when repeated for emphasis.

> *Example*: These are very understandable words—safe words—sane words.

(5) Between the subject and the subject-matter; or between the subject-matter and the authority.

> *Examples*: COTTON.—For the cotton season 1914-15 there will be shown a decided increase in exportation to Continental and Mediterranean ports.
>
> Nothing ever becomes real till it is experienced; even a proverb is no proverb to you, till life has illustrated it.—*Keats*.

(6) To separate an independent clause interjected into a sentence.

> *Example*: I may get strong and well again—I think I will—but if I don't (etc.)

(7) After a colon, when a long quotation is introduced.

> *Example*: Dinner being over, the President arose and read the following address :—

A dash is used after other punctuation marks when a longer pause than they denote is required.

When two hyphens are used by the typist to indicate a dash, they may be joined into a continuous line by using a pen or sharp-pointed pencil; or the additional character will be supplied by the typewriter company.

Hyphen

Is used:

(1) Between compound words.

> *Examples*: half-time
> world-famed
> world-wide
> first-class
> laughter-loving
> twenty-three
> forget-me-not
> Vice-President
> income-yielding
> self-supporting

(2) To divide words at the end of a line. The division should be made between syllables.

> *Example*: "The sun had set, the day was done, the shadows of evening were falling."

(3)   To distinguish words of similar spelling but different meaning.

Examples: Restored   re-stored
Reformed   re-formed

(4)   Instead of the dieresis, to indicate that two adjacent vowels do not unite to form a dipthong.

Examples: co-ordinate
co-operation
re-elect

PARENTHESIS

Used to enclose:

(1)   Any expression which breaks the continuity of the sentence and which is independent in its construction.

Examples: These fasteners may be bought (I think they cost but ten cents) at any stationer's.

He arrived (God Bless Him!) in the knick of time.

If the parenthetical matter is complete in sense, punctuation-marks should be included in the parenthesis; as, You promised (did you not?) to remit on or before the first.

(2)   An explanatory word or phrase.

Examples: This street (Main Street) runs north and south.

Mrs. L. Smith (née Carroll) was enrolled.

(3) Enumerations.

Examples:
- **(1) Office supplies**
- **(2) Rent**
- **(3) Telephone & Telegrams**
- **(a) Traffic Department**
- **(b) Transportation Department**

(4) A question-mark used after an assertion to throw doubt upon it.

Example: She says she is an expert (?) stenographer.

It would similarly enclose an exclamation-mark used to express wonder:

Example: They have already written 800 (!) envelopes, and stamped them too.

BRACKETS
Used instead of parentheses.

BRACKET OR BRACE
Used to connect several terms or items.

CARET
Used to show where interlined words are to be inserted. The typist may use a combination of the underscore and fraction-mark, as shown here:

```
              it
Why is/that so many
```

Dieresis

Placed over the second of two successive vowels to show they do not form a diphthong but are pronounced separately. *aëronaut, zoölogy.*

Asterisk

Used to indicate a reference or an ellipsis.

Daggers

Reference marks connecting words in the text with marginal notes or footnotes.

Paragraph.

Used in printers' "copy" or shorthand notes to indicate a new paragraph. (*X* or two vertical parallel lines || are also used by shorthand-writers to indicate a paragraph.)

Section

(Combination of two s's). Placed before subdivisions of books to facilitate reference.

Breve

Denotes the short sound of a vowel. *Căt.*

Macron

Denotes the long sound of a vowel. *Hāte.*

Ditto

(The same).   Denotes words or figures are to be supplied from the line above.

Cedilla

A mark placed under the letter *c* in certain French words commonly used in English, to show it has the sound of s. *façade.*

Tilde —(or filde)

Mark placed over the letter *n* in certain Spanish words commonly used in English to show it has the sound of *ny* —*cañon* (pronounced kanyon). *Señor.*

Quit Claim Deed.   See *Deeds.*

Railroad Securities.   Stocks and bonds of railroads.   When investing in them, earning capacity, physical condition, management, financing or indebtedness, how secured, whether legal for savings banks, and density of population in section traversed, are vital factors to be taken into consideration.

Rebate.   An allowance or discount.

Receipt.   An admission in writing that something has been received.

A creditor is not obliged to give a receipt; it is a mere act of courtesy.

New York,_____ 190___

Received from_____

_____ Dollars

$_____ _____

FORM OF RECEIPT.

$100.   NEW YORK,_____May 1,____1916__

Received of_Henry Jones_ - - - - -

One Hundred 00/100 - - - - - - - -DOLLARS,

IN FULL OF ALL DEMANDS AGAINST HIM.

Charles Brown

RECEIPT IN FULL.

$50.   NEW YORK,_____Jan. 1,____1916__

Received of_Joseph Shaw_ - - - - -

Fifty 00/100 - - - - - - - - - DOLLARS

TO APPLY ON ACCOUNT.

Sarah Smith

RECEIPT ON ACCOUNT.

Receiver.   A person appointed by a court to administer the affairs of an insolvent company, or to distribute the property of a dissolved company.

Registered Bond.   See *Bonds and Stocks.*

Release.   To discharge or acquit from obligation. The paper or instrument in which a right or claim is renounced.

Form of General Release.

To all to whom these Presents shall come or may concern, greeting; know ye, *That....................................... for and in consideration of the sum of......................Dollars lawful money of the United States of America, to.............in hand paid by.. the receipt whereof is hereby acknowledged, have remised, released and forever discharged and by these Presents do for...................... heirs, executors and administrators, remise, release and forever discharge the said......................heirs, executors and administrators, of all and from all, and all manner of action and actions, cause and causes of actions, suits, debts, dues, sums of money, accounts, reckonings, bonds, bills, specialties, covenants, contracts, controversies, agreements, promises, variances, trespasses, damages, judgments, extents, executions, claims and demands whatsoever in law or in equity, which against.................................ever had, now ha....or which heirs, executors or administrators, hereafter can, shall or may have for, upon or by reason of any matter, cause or thing whatsoever from the beginning of the world to the day of the date of these presents.*

In Witness Whereof, ...*have hereunto set........hand....and seal......the...................day of....................in the year of our Lord one thousand nine hundred and.........................*

Sealed and Delivered in the Presence of

Release of Dower.   The release by a widow of her one-third life interest in the estate of her husband.

192

Form of Release of Dower.

Know all Men by these Presents *that I, ...*
of the town of............, wife of........(or widow of..........),
late of said town, deceased, party of the first part, in consideration of
........................Dollars to me paid by....................of
the said town of...........................party of the second part,
the receipt whereof is hereby acknowledged, have granted, remised, re-
leased, conveyed and forever quit-claim, and by these presents do grant,
remise, release, and forever quit-claim unto the said.................
and to his heirs and assigns forever, all the dower and thirds, and all
other right, title, interest, property, claim and demand whatsoever, in
law and in equity, of me, the said....................of, in and to,
All *that certain piece, parcel or lot of land, situate lying and being*
in the town of.........................and bounded and described as
follows :

(here is inserted description of property)

So that neither I, the said......................., my heirs, executors,
administrators and assigns, nor any other person or persons for me, them
or any of them, shall have claim or demand any dower or thirds, or any
other right, title, claim or demand, of, in, or to the same, or any part
thereof, but thereof and therefrom shall be utterly barred and excluded
forever.

In Witness Whereof *I have hereunto set my hand and seal this*
...................day of...................in the year..............

Sealed and Delivered in Presence of
  (*witnesses*)   (SEAL)

Rights. Stockholders are usually given the RIGHT to subscribe to any new stock the company may issue. If the company is one of the large and prosperous ones, these rights are in great demand and are bought and sold the same as stock.

Rolling Stock. Stock of a railroad on wheels—locomotives, freight and passenger cars, hand cars, etc.

Roman	I	1	XX	20
Numerals.	II	2	XXX	30
	III	3	XL	40
	IV	4	L	50
	V	5	LX	60
	VI	6	LXX	70
	VII	7	LXXX	80
	VIII	8	XC	90
	IX	9	C	100
	X	10	CC	200
	XI	11	CCC	300
	XII	12	CCCC	400
	XIII	13	D	500
	XIV	14	DC	600
	XV	15	DCC	700
	XVI	16	DCCC	800
	XVII	17	CM	900
	XVIII	18	M	1000
	XIX	19		

Royalties. Proportion of revenue paid to an author or inventor for the right to use his work, or the revenue paid to the owner of land for the privilege of operating his property, as in the case of oil wells, mines, etc.

Sabotage. An attempt to coerce or attain an object by working with intentional incompetency.

Salvage. The allowance or compensation made by the owners for assistance rendered their vessel while in distress, or for recovering it after it has been lost.

Satisfaction.   A written acknowledgment that an indebtedness or obligation has been paid.

Savings   A bank organized under the state laws, or
Bank.   under the Federal laws if in the District of
Columbia, for the purpose of receiving deposits, the intent being that such deposits shall largely be the savings of the small earners, such as laborers, wage earners, and small-salaried persons in general, who are not expected to be in a position to invest money intelligently for themselves, and whose savings are so small that no adequate form of investment can easily be found. The aggregate of these savings in any one bank is supposed to be invested by an intelligent board of men elected for the purpose, usually called the "Board of Investment" or "Finance Committee." The legal restrictions placed upon the investment of "savings bank" funds vary greatly in different states, some being very strict and conservative and properly safeguarding the interest of depositors; others woefully lax and unsafe.   *   *   *   Interest ranging from 3% to 5% according to the bank is paid on money deposited, in accordance of course with the rules and regulations of the institution.—(*Extract from "Municipal and Corporation Bonds" by Montgomery Rollins.*)

Scrip.   Certificate for a fraction of a share of stock. Temporary certificate.

Second   See *Mortgage.*
Mortgage.

Securities. See *Investments.*

Semi-Annual. Twice a year. J-J (January-July); F-A (February-August); M-S (March-September); A-O (April-October); M-N (May-November); J-D (June-December).

Serial Rights. The right to publish an article serially or in instalments in a magazine, newspaper or other issue published in consecutive order.

Sherman Law. Under the following anti-trust law, the Standard Oil Co., Tobacco Trust and others were dissolved:

Be it enacted by the Senate and House of Representatives of the United States of America in Congress assembled:

SEC. 1. Every contract, combination in the form of trust or otherwise, or conspiracy, in restraint of trade or commerce among the several States, or with foreign nations, is hereby declared to be illegal. Every person who shall make any such contract, or engage in any such combination or conspiracy, shall be deemed guilty of a misdemeanor, and, on conviction thereof, shall be punished by a fine not exceeding $5,000, or by imprisonment not exceeding one year, or by both said punishments in the discretion of the Court.

SEC. 2. Every person who shall monopolize, or attempt to monopolize, or combine or conspire with any other person or persons to monopolize any part of the trade or commerce among the several States, or with foreign nations, shall be deemed guilty of a misdemeanor, and on conviction thereof, shall be punished by fine not exceeding $5,000, or by imprisonment not exceeding one year, or by both said punishments, in the discretion of the Court.

SEC. 3. Every contract, combination in form or trust or otherwise, or conspiracy, in restrain of trade or commerce in any Territory of the United States, or the District of Columbia, or in restraint of trade or commerce between any such Territory and another, or between any such Territory or Territories and State or States or the District of Columbia, or with foreign nations, or between the District of Columbia and any State or States or foreign nations, is hereby declared illegal. Every person who shall make any such contract, or engage in any such combination or conspiracy, shall be deemed guilty of a misdemeanor, and on conviction thereof, shall be punished by fine not exceeding $5,000, or by imprisonment not exceeding one year, or by both said punishments in the discretion of the Court.

SEC. 4. The several Circuit Courts of the United States are hereby invested with jurisdiction to prevent and restrain violations of this act; and it shall be the duty of the several District Attorneys of the United States, in their respective districts, under the direction of the Attorney General, to institute proceedings in equity to prevent and restrain such violations. Such proceedings may be by way of petition setting forth the case and praying that such violation shall be enjoined or otherwise prohibited. When the parties complained of shall have been duly notified of such petition the Court shall proceed, as soon as may be, to the hearing and determination of the case; and pending such petition and before final decree, the Court may at any time make such temporary restraining order or prohibition as shall be deemed just in the premises.

SEC. 5. Whenever it shall appear to the Court before which any proceeding under sec. 4 of this act may be pending, that the ends of justice require that other parties should be brought before the Court, the Court may cause them to be summoned, whether they reside in the district in which the Court is held or not; and subpoenas to that end may be served in any district by the marshal thereof.

SEC. 6. Any property owned under any contract or by any combination, or pursuant to any conspiracy (and being the subject thereof) mentioned in sec. 1 of this act, and being in the course of transportation from one State to another, or to a foreign country, shall be forfeited to the United States, and may be seized and condemned by like proceedings as those provided by law for the forfeiture, seizure and condemnation of property imported into the United States contrary to law.

SEC. 7. Any person who shall be injured in his business or property by any other person or corporation by reason of anything forbidden or declared to be unlawful by this act may sue therefor in any Circuit Court of the United States in the district in which the defendant resides or is found, without respect to the amount in controversy, and shall recover threefold the damages by him sustained, and the costs of suit, including a reasonable attorney's fee.

SEC. 8. That the word "person" or "persons" wherever used in this act shall be deemed to include corporations and associations existing under or authorized by the laws of either the United States, the laws of any of the Territories, the laws of any State or the laws of any foreign country.

Approved July 2, 1890.

Sic.   So; thus.

Signing by Mark.   An illiterate person who cannot sign his or her name signs "by mark"; that is, his or her name is written by another, the illiterate making the mark "X" and the words "His (Her) Mark" are written above and below it, i. e.,

$$Her$$

$$Mary \quad X \quad Smith$$

$$Mark$$

It is necessary to have two witnesses attest such a signature.

Sine Die.   Without date.

Sine Qua Non.   Indispensable condition.

Sinking Fund. A fund set apart from earnings to redeem the securities of a company when they become due or to take up obligations.

Site. Piece of land. Location.

Solvent. Able to meet debts and obligations.

Specie. Gold or silver money. Coins.

Speed Records.

Steam Locomotive ....115 Miles per hour
Aeroplane ....106 " " "
Automobile ....106 " " "
Electric Locomotive .... 90 " " "
Motorcycle .... 83 " " "
Motor Boat .... 54 " " "
Dirigible .... 45 " " "
Steamship (passenger) .... 32 " " "
(Subject to change)

Spot Cash. Merchandise to be paid for on delivery; sent "C. O. D." (Cash or Collect on Delivery).

Spot Price. The day's price.

Standard of Weight and Fineness. The standard of "fineness" for gold and silver coins is defined as follows in the law of 1873 (R S 3514): "The standard for both gold and silver coins of the United States shall be such that of one thousand parts by weight nine hundred shall be of pure metal and one hundred of alloy. The alloy of the gold coins shall be of copper, or of copper and silver; but the silver shall in no case exceed one-tenth of the whole alloy.''

In the actual making of coins there is slight variation from the Standard values and tolerances or allowable errors are also established. The "standard" however refers only to the correct or ideal values. The Standard weights of the coins are as follows:

Gold Coins	Amount	$20.00	Weight	Grains	516
	"	10.00	"	"	258
	"	5.00	"	"	129
	"	2.50	"	"	64.5
Silver Coins	"	1.00	"	"	412.5
	"	.50	"	"	192.9
		.25	"	"	96.45
		.10	"	"	38.58
Minor Coins	"	.05	"	"	77.16
		.01	"	"	48.

See *Sterling.*

Standard Time. See *Difference in Time.*

Status Quo. The existing state.

Statutes of Limitation. See *Debts* and *Interest.*

Sterling. The standard of fineness for gold and silver coins as defined by British law. The standard for gold coins is, pure metal .916, or 11/12, and of silver .925. Anything made of STERLING silver conforms to this ratio of 92½ silver to 7½% alloy.   Also meaning true, genuine, fine, as a STERLING character.

Stock Exchange.   The definition of a stock exchange given by the Congressional Committee which investigated the Exchange is: "A stock exchange is a market or meeting place controlled by rules on which only members are permitted to deal with one another on their own behalf, or for their customers, where securities of corporations are bought and sold.   Manifestly, a security privileged to be bought and sold on such exchange obtains a wider market and a more definite current value than one which is not."

The New York Stock Exchange was organized in 1817.

The Hughes Commission, in its report dated June 7, 1909, describes the functions of the New York Stock Exchange as follows:

"The New York Stock Exchange is a voluntary organization limited to 1,100 members, of whom about 700 are active, some of them residents of other cities.   Memberships are sold for about $80,000.   The Exchange as such does no business, merely providing facilities to members and regulating their conduct.   The governing power is in an elected committee of forty members and is plenary in scope.   The business transacted on the floor is the purchase and sale of stocks and bonds of corporations and governments.   Practically all transactions must be completed by delivery and payment on the following day.

The mechanism of the Exchange, provided by its constitution and rules, is the evolution of more than a century.   An organization of stock-brokers existed here in 1792, acquiring more definite form in 1817.   It seems certain that for a long period the members were brokers or agents only; at the present time many are principals as well as agents, trading for themselves as well as for their customers. A number of prominent capitalists hold membership merely for the purpose of availing themselves of the reduced commission charge which the rules authorize between members.

The volume of transactions indicates that the Exchange is today probably the most important financial institution in the world. * * *"

NAMES OF FOREIGN EXCHANGES.

Paris ....Bourse de Paris
Germany ....Der Berliner Börse
Spain ....Bolsa Nacional, Madrid
Russia ....Berscha, Petrograd

Stocks and Bonds.   See *Bonds and Stocks.*

Stockholders.   Those who have invested funds in the shares of a company. In case of the failure of the company, stockholders usually cannot be held liable for more than the amount of their shares. See *Bonds and Stocks.*

Stop Order.   An order to a broker to sell when a stock reaches a certain price. An order on a bank to stop payment of a check.

Subject to Sale.   Offering made with understanding it is not binding if sale is made to another in the meantime.

Subpoena.   A writ commanding a person to appear to give testimony.

Subsidiary Company.   A subordinate or affiliated company.

Subsidy. Assistance given by a government to public utility companies or others, in the expectation it will redound to the benefit of the general public.

Sunday Contracts. All contracts made on Sunday are void, except those for works of charity or necessity.

Deeds, notes and checks made on Sunday are void; they may be dated ahead or on Monday. See *Business Laws.*

Surety. A guaranty or security against loss, or for the carrying out of some agreed promise or act. A person (or company) who so guarantees another acts as "surety" and any paper or bond given as evidence of the fact bears the same title. A surety company is one, which, for proper compensation, acts as "surety."—(*From "Municipal and Corporation Bonds," by Montgomery Rollins.*)

Syndicate. A group of men, bankers or any combination of the same who unite their mutual interests for the purchase or control of certain properties or securities. The members of the syndicate are generally bound by what is called a "syndicate agreement," in other words a written instrument to carry out the terms of the agreement signed by the parties. Some person, firm, bank or trust company is usually selected as a "syndicate manager" whose duty it is to see that the terms of the "syndicate agreement" are fulfilled by all parties.—(*From "Municipal and Corporation Bonds," by Montgomery Rollins.*)

Synonyms. (Crabb's Synonyms, Harper & Brothers.)

ABANDON—desert, forsake, relinquish, resign, renounce, abdicate

ABASE—humble, degrade, disgrace, debase

ABASH—confound, confuse

ABATE—lessen, diminish, decrease

ABHOR—detest, abominate, loathe

ABILITY—dexterity, address

ABLE—capable, capacious

ABJURE—recant, retract, revoke, recall

ABOLISH—abrogate, repeal, revoke, annul, cancel

ABOMINATE—detest, execrate

ABOVE—over, upon, beyond

ABRIDGE—curtail, contract

ABRIDGMENT — compendium, epitome, digest, summary, abstract

ABRUPT—rugged, rough

ABSCOND—steal away, secrete one's self

ABSENT—abstracted, abstract, diverted, distracted

ABSOLVE—acquit, clear

ABSOLUTE—despotic, arbitrary, tyrannical

ABSORB—swallow up, ingulf, engross, imbibe

ABSTAIN—forbear, refrain

ABSTINENCE—fast

ABSTINENT—sober, abstemious, temperate

ABSTRACT—separate, distinguish

ABSTRACTION—alienation, estrangement

ABUSE—misuse

ABUSE—invective

ACCEPTABLE—grateful, welcome

ACCEPTANCE—acceptation

ACCIDENT — chance, contingency, casualty

ACCIDENTAL—incidental, casual, contingent

ACCOMPANIMENT—companion, concomitant

ACCOMPANY—attend, escort

ACCOMPLISH—effect, execute, achieve

ACCOMPLISH—perfect

ACCOST—salute, address, greet, hail, welcome

ACCOUNT—reckoning, bill, narrative, description

ACCURATE—exact, precise

ACCUSE—charge, impeach, arraign

ACCUSE—censure

ACKNOWLEDGE—own, confess, avow

ACQUAINTANCE—familiarity, intimacy

ACQUIRE—obtain, gain, win, earn, attain

ACQUIREMENT—acquisition

ACRIMONY—tartness, asperity, harshness

ACT—do, make, work, operate, action, deed

ACTION — gesture, gesticulation, posture, attitude

ACTIVE—diligent, industrious, assiduous, laborious, brisk, agile, nimble, busy, officious

ACTOR—agent, player, performer

ACTUAL—real, positive

ACTUATE—impel, induce

ACUTE—keen, shrewd

ADD—join, unite, coalesce

ADDICT—devote, apply

ADDRESS—apply, speech, harangue, oration

ADDUCE—allege, assign, advance

ADHERE—attach

ADHESION—adherence

ADJACENT—adjoining, contiguous

ADMIT—receive, allow, permit, suffer, tolerate, grant

ADMITTANCE—admission

ADMONISH—advise

ADMONITION—warning, caution

ADORE—worship, reverence, venerate, revere

ADORN—decorate, embellish

ADULATE—flatter, compliment

ADVANCE—proceed

ADVANTAGE—benefit, utility, profit

ADVERSE—contrary, opposite, inimical, hostile, repugnant, averse

ADVERSITY—distress

ADVERTISE—publish

ADVICE—counsel, instruction

AFFABLE—courteous

AFFAIR—business, concern

AFFECT—concern, assume, pretend

AFFECTED—disposed

AFFECTION—love

AFFECTIONATE—kind, fond

AFFIRM—asseverate, assure, vouch, aver, protest, assert

AFFIX—subjoin, attach, annex

AFFLICT—distress, trouble

AFFLICTION—grief, sorrow

AFFORD—yield, produce

AFFORD—spare

AFRAID—fearful, timorous, timid

AFTER—behind

AGGRAVATE—irritate, provoke, exasperate, tantalize

AGGRESSOR—assailant

AGITATION—trepidation, tremor, emotion

AGREE—accede, consent, comply, acquiesce

AGREE—accord, suit, coincide, concur

AGREEABLE—pleasant, pleasing

AGREEMENT—contract, covenant, compact, bargain

AIM—object, end, view

AIM—point, level, aspire

AIR—manner, mien, look

ALARM—terror, fright, consternation

ALERTNESS—alacrity

ALL—whole, every, each

ALLAY—soothe, appease, mitigate, assuage

ALLEVIATE—relieve

ALLIANCE — league, confederacy, affinity

ALLOT—appoint, destine

ALLOW—grant, bestow

ALLOWANCE — stipend, salary, wages, hire, pay

ALLUDE—refer, hint, suggest

ALLURE—tempt, seduce, entice, decoy

ALLY—confederate

ALONE—solitary, lonely

ALSO—likewise, too

ALWAYS—at all times, ever

AMBASSADOR—envoy, plenipotentiary, deputy

AMBIGUOUS—equivocal

AMEND—correct, emend, improve, mend, better

AMIABLE—lovely, beloved

AMICABLE—friendly

AMOROUS—loving, fond

AMPLE—spacious, capacious

AMUSE—divert, entertain, beguile

AMUSEMENT—entertainment, diversion, sport, recreation, pastime

ANECDOTE—story, memoir, chronicle, annal

ANGER—resentment, wrath, ire, indignation, choler, rage, fury

ANIMADVERSION—criticism, stricture

ANIMAL—brute, beast

ANIMATE—inspire, enliven, cheer, exhilarate

ANNOUNCE—proclaim, publish

ANSWER—reply, rejoinder, response

ANSWERABLE—responsible, accountable, amenable

ANTECEDENT—preceding, foregoing, previous, anterior, prior, former

APOLOGIZE—defend, justify, exculpate, excuse, plead

APPAREL—attire, array

APPARENT—visible, clear, plain, obvious, evident, manifest

APPEARANCE—air, aspect

APPEASE—calm, pacify, quiet, still

APPLAUSE—acclamation

APPOINT—order, prescribe, ordain

APPRAISE — appreciate, estimate, esteem

APPREHEND—conceive, suppose, imagine, fear, dread

APPROACH—access, admittance, approximate

APPROPRIATE—usurp, abrogate, assume, ascribe

ARCHITECT—builder

ARGUE—dispute, debate, evince, prove

ARGUMENT—reason, proof

ARISE—mount, ascend, climb, scale, proceed, issue, spring, flow, emanate

ARMS—weapons

ARMY—host

ARROGANCE—presumption

ART—cunning, deceit

ARTFUL—artificial, fictitious

ARTICLE—condition, term

ARTIFICE—trick, finesse, stratagem

ARTIST—artisan, artificer, mechanic

ASCRIBE—impute, attribute

ASK—beg, request, claim, demand, inquire, question, interrogate

ASPERSE—detract, defame, slander, calumniate

ASSEMBLE—muster, collect, convene, convoke

ASSEMBLY—assemblage, group, collection, company, meeting, congregation, parliament, diet, congress, convention, synod, convocation, council

ASSENT—consent, approbation, concurrence

ASSERT—maintain, vindicate

ASSOCIATE—companion

ASSOCIATION—society, company, partnership, combination

ASSURANCE—confidence, impudence

ASTRONOMY—astrology

ASYLUM—refuge, shelter, retreat

ATONE FOR—expiate

ATTACHMENT—affection, inclination

ATTACK—assail, assault, encounter, onset, charge

ATTEMPT—trial, endeavor, effort, essay, undertaking, enterprise

ATTEND TO—mind, regard, heed, notice, wait on, hearken, listen

ATTENTION—application, study

ATTENTIVE—careful

ATTRACT—allure, invite, engage

ATTRACTIONS—allurements, charms

AUDACITY—effrontery, hardihood or hardiness, boldness

AUGUR—presage, forebode, betoken, portend

AUSPICIOUS—propitious

AUSTERE—rigid, severe, rigorous, stern

AVARICIOUS — miserly, parsimonious, niggardly

AVENGE—revenge, vindicate

AVERSE—unwilling, backward, loath, reluctant

AVERSION—antipathy, dislike, hatred, repugnance

AVIDITY—greediness, eagerness

AVOID—eschew, shun. elude

AWAKEN—excite, provoke, rouse, stir up

AWARE—on one's guard, apprised, conscious

AWE—reverence, dread

AWKWARD—clumsy, cross, untoward, crooked, forward, perverse

AXIOM—maxim, aphorism, apophthegm, saying, adage, proverb, by-word, saw

BABBLE—chatter, chat, prattle, prate

BACK—backward, behind

BAD—wicked, evil

BADLY—ill

BAFFLE—defeat, discontent, confound

BAND—company, crew, gang

BANE—pest, ruin

BANISH—exile, expel

BARE—naked, uncovered, scanty, destitute, mere

BASE—vile, mean

BATTLE—combat, engagements, action

BE—exist, subsist, become, grow

BEAR—yield, carry, convey, transport, suffer, endure, support

BEAT—strike, hit, defeat, overpower, rout, overthrow

BEATIFICATION—canonization

BEAUTIFUL—fine, handsome, pretty

BECOMING—decent, seemly, fit, suitable, comely, graceful

BEG—desire, beseech, solicit, entreat, supplicate, implore, crave

BEGIN—commence, enter upon

BEHAVIOR—conduct, carriage, deportment, demeanor

BELIEF—credit, trust, faith

BEND—bent

BENEFACTION—donation

BENEFICIENT—bountiful, bounteous, munificent, generous, liberal

BENEFIT—favor, kindness, civility

BENEFIT—service, good office

BENEVOLENCE—beneficence, benignity, humanity, kindness, tenderness

BENT—curved, crooked, awry, bias, inclination, prepossession

BEREAVE—deprive, strip

BESIDES—moreover, except

BEWAIL—bemoan, lament

BIAS—prepossession, prejudice

BIND—tie, oblige, engage

BISHOPRIC—diocese

BLAME—censure, condemn, reprove, reproach, upbraid

BLAMELESS—irreproachable, unblemished, unspotted, or spotless

BLEMISH—stain, spot, speck, flaw, defect, fault

BLOT OUT—expunge, rase or erase, efface, cancel, obliterate

BLOW—stroke

BODY—corpse, carcass

BOLD—fearless, intrepid, undaunted

BOOTY—spoil, prey

BORDER—edge, rim, or brim, brink, margin, verge, boundary, frontier, confine, precinct

BOUND—limit, confine, circumscribe, restrict

BOUNDLESS—unbounded, unlimited, infinite

BOUNDS—boundary

BRAVE—gallant, defy, dare, challenge

BRAVERY—courage, valor

BREACH—break, gap, chasm

BREAK—rack, rend, tear, bruise, squeeze, pound, crush, burst, crack, split

BREED—engender

BREEZE—gale, blast, gust, storm, tempest, hurricane

BRIGHTNESS—lustre, splendor, brilliancy

BRING—fetch, carry

BUILD—erect, construct

BULKY—massive

BURIAL—interment, sepulture

BUSINESS—occupation, employment, engagement, avocation, trade, profession, art, office, duty

BUSTLE—tumult, uproar

BUY—purchase, bargain, cheapen

CALAMITY—disaster, misfortune, mischance, mishap

CALCULATE—reckon, compute, count

CALENDAR—almanac, ephemeris

CALL—cry, exclaim, invite, bid, summon

CALM—composed, collected, placid, serene

CAN—may

CANDID—open, sincere

CAPACITY—capaciousness

CAPTIOUS—cross, peevish, petulant, fretful

CAPTURE—seizure, prize

CARE—solicitude, anxiety, concern, regard, charge, management

CAREFUL—cautious, provident

CARESS—fondle

CARNAGE — slaughter, massacre, butchery

CARRIAGE—gait, walk

CASE—cause

CAST—throw, hurl, turn, description

CAUSE—reason, motive, occasion, create

CAUTIOUS—wary, circumspect

CEASE—leave off, discontinue

CELEBRATE—commemorate

CELESTIAL—heavenly

CENSURE—animadvert, criticise

CENSURE—carp, cavil

CERTAIN—sure, secure

CESSATION—stop, rest, intermission

CHAIN—fetter, band, shackle

CHANCE—fortune, fate, probability, hazard

CHANGE—alter, vary, exchange, barter, substitute, variation, vicissitude

CHANGEABLE—mutable, variable, inconsistent, fickle, versatile

CHARACTER—reputation

CHARM—enchant, fascinate, enrapture, captivate

CHASTEN—to chastise

CHASTITY—continence

CHEAT—defraud, trick

CHECK—curb, control, rebuff, reprimand, reprove, rebuke, stop

CHEER—encourage, comfort

CHEERFUL—merry, sprightly, gay

CHIEF—principal, main, leader, chieftain, head

CHILDISH—infantine

CHILL—cold

CHOOSE—prefer, pick, select, elect
CIRCLE—sphere, orb, globe
CIRCUIT—tour, round
CIRCUMSCRIBE—inclose
CIRCUMSTANCE—incident, fact
CIRCUMSTANTIAL—particular, minute
CITE—quote, summon
CIVIL—polite, obliging, complaisant
CLANDESTINE—secret
CLASP—hug, embrace
CLASS—order, rank, degree, arrange, range
CLEAN—cleanly, pure
CLEAR—lucid, bright, vivid
CLEARLY—distinctly
CLEARNESS—perspicuity
CLEMENCY—lenity, mercy
CLERGYMAN—parson, priest, minister
CLEVER—skillful, expert, dexterous, adroit
CLOAK—mask, blind, veil
CLOG—load, encumber
CLOISTER—convent, monastery
CLOSE—compact, near, nigh, shut, conclude, finish
COADJUTER—assistant
COARSE—rough, rude
COAX—wheedle, cajole, fawn
COERCE—restrain
COEVAL—contemporary
COGENT—forcible, strong
COLLEAGUE—partner
COLOR—dye, tinge, stain, hue, tint
COLORABLE—specious, ostensible, plausible, feasible
COMBAT—oppose
COMBATANT—champion
COMBINATION—cabal, plot, conspiracy

COME—arrive
COMFORT—pleasure
COMMAND—order, injunction, precept
COMMANDING—imperative, imperious, authoritative
COMMISSION—authorize, empower
COMMODIOUS—convenient
COMMODITY—goods, merchandise, ware
COMMON—vulgar, ordinary, mean
COMMONLY—generally, frequently, usually
COMMOTION—disturbance
COMMUNICATE—impart
COMMUNION—converse
COMMUNITY—society
COMPARISON—contrast
COMPATIBLE—consistent
COMPEL—force, oblige, necessitate
COMPENSATION—amends, satisfaction, recompense, remuneration, requital, reward
COMPETENT—fitted, qualified
COMPETITION—emulation, rivalry
COMPLAIN—lament, regret, murmur, repine
COMPLAINT—accusation
COMPLAISANCE—deference, condescension
COMPLETE—perfect, finished
COMPLEXITY—complication, intricacy
COMPLY—conform, yield, submit
COMPLIANT—yielding, submissive
COMPOSE—settle
COMPOSED—sedate
COMPOUND—complex, compose
COMPREHENSIVE—extensive
COMPRISE—comprehend, embrace contain, include
CONCEAL—dissemble, disguise, hide secrete

CONCEALMENT—secrecy
CONCEIT—fancy
CONCEIVE—understand, comprehend
CONCEPTION—notion
CONCERT—contrive, manage
CONCILIATE—reconcile
CONCLUSION—inference, deduction
CONCLUSIVE—decisive, convincing
CONCORD—harmony
CONDITION—station
CONDUCE—contribute
CONDUCT—manage, direct
CONFEDERATE—accomplice
CONFER—bestow
CONFIDE—trust
CONFIDENT—dogmatical, positive
CONFINEMENT—imprisonment, captivity
CONFIRM—establish
CONFLICT—combat, contest
CONFORMABLE—agreeable, suitable
CONFOUND—confuse
CONFRONT—face
CONFUSION—disorder
CONFUTE—refute, disprove, oppugn
CONJECTURE—supposition, surmise
CONJUNCTURE—crisis
CONNECT—combine, unite
CONNECTION—relation
CONQUER—vanquish, subdue, overcome, surmount
CONQUERER—victor
CONSCIENTIOUS—scrupulous
CONSENT—permit, allow
CONSEQUENCE—effect, result, issue, event
CONSIDER—reflect
CONSIDERATION—reason
CONSIGN—commit, intrust
CONSOLE—solace, comfort
CONSONANT—accordant, consistent

CONSTANCY—stability, steadiness, firmness
CONSTITUTE—appoint, depute
CONSTRAINT—compulsion, restraint
CONSULT—deliberate
CONSUMMATION—completion
CONTACT—touch
CONTAGION—infection
CONTAGIOUS—epidemical, pestilential
CONTAIN—hold
CONTAMINATE—defile, pollute, taint, corrupt
CONTEMN—despise, scorn, disdain
CONTEMPLATE—mediate, muse
CONTEMPTIBLE—contemptuous, despicable, pitiful
CONTEMPTUOUS—scornful, disdainful
CONTEND—contest, dispute
CONTENTMENT—satisfaction
CONTINUAL—perpetual, constant
CONTINUAL—continued
CONTINUANCE—continuation, duration, continuity
CONTINUE—remain, stay, persevere, persist, pursue, prosecute
CONTRACTED—confined, narrow
CONTRADICT—deny, oppose
CONTRIVE—devise, invent
CONTROVERT—dispute
CONTUMACY—rebellion
CONVENIENT—suitable
CONVERSANT—familiar
CONVERSATION—dialogue, conference, colloquy
CONVERT—proselyte
CONVICT—detect, convince, persuade
CONVIVIAL—social
COOL—cold, frigid
COPY—transcribe, model, pattern, specimen

Coquet—jilt

Corner—angle

Corporal—corporeal, bodily, material

Corpulent—stout, lusty

Correct—rectify, reform, accurate

Correction — discipline, punishment

Correspondent—answerable, suitable

Cost—expense, price, charge

Cover—hide, shelter, screen

Covetousness—cupidity, avarice

Countenance—sanction, support

Countryman — peasant, swain, hind, rustic, clown

Couple—pair, brace

Courage—fortitude, resolution

Course—race, passage

Courteous—complaisant, courtly

Credit—favor, influence

Crime—vice, sin, misdemeanor

Criminal—guilty, culprit, malefactor, felon, convict

Criterion—standard

Cruel—inhuman, barbarous, brutal, savage

Cry—weep, scream, shriek

Culpable—faulty

Cultivation—culture, civilization, refinement, tillage, husbandry

Cunning—crafty, subtle, sly, wily

Cure—heal, remedy

Curious—inquisitive, prying

Cursory—hasty, slight, desultory

Custom—habit, fashion, manner, practice

Daily—diurnal

Dainty—delicacy

Danger—peril, hazard

Daring—bold

Dark—obscure, dim, mysterious

Deadly—mortal, fatal

Deal—quantity, portion

Death—departure, decease, demise

Debate—deliberate

Debility—infirmity, imbecility

Debt—due

Decay—decline, consumption

Deceit—deception, fraud, guile

Deceive—delude, impose upon

Deceiver—impostor

Decency—decorum

Decide—determine, conclude upon

Decided—determined, resolute, decisive

Declaim—inveigh

Decree—edict, proclamation

Dedicate—devote, consecrate, hallow

Deduct—subtract

Deduction—abatement

Deed—exploit, achievement, feat

Deface—disfigure, deform

Defeat—foil, disappoint, frustrate

Defection—revolt

Defective—deficient

Defend—protect, vindicate

Defendant—defender

Defender—advocate, pleader

Defensible—defensive

Definite—positive

Definition—explanation

Deity—divinity

Dejection — depression, melancholy

Delay—defer, postpone, procrastinate, prolong, protract, retard

Delegate—depute, delegate, deputy

Delightful—charming

Delineate—sketch

DELIVER—rescue, save

DELIVERANCE—delivery

DEMAND—require

DEMOLISH—raze, dismantle, destroy

DEMUR—hesitate, pause, doubt, hesitation, objection

DENOTE—signify

DENY—refuse

DEPENDENCE—reliance

DEPLORE—lament

DEPONENT—evidence, witness

DEPOSIT—pledge, security

DEPRAVITY — depravation, corruption

DEPREDATION—robbery

DEPRIVE—debar, abridge

DEPTH—profundity

DERANGEMENT — insanity, lunacy, madness, mania

DERIDE—mock, ridicule, rally, banter

DERIVE—trace, deduce

DESERT—merit, worth

DESIGN—purpose, intend, mean, plan, scheme, project

DESIRE—wish, long for, hanker after, covet

DESIST—leave off

DESPAIR — desperation, despondency

DESPERATE—hopeless

DESTINY—fate, lot, doom, destination

DESTROY—consume, waste

DESTRUCTION—ruin

DESTRUCTIVE—ruinous, pernicious

DETECT—discover

DETERMINE—resolve

DEVIATE—wander, swerve, stray

DEVIL—demon

DEVISE—bequeath

DICTATE—prescribe, suggestion

DICTION—style, phrase, phraseology

DICTIONARY — encyclopædia, lexicon, vocabulary, glossary, nomenclature

DIE—expire

DIFFER—vary, disagree, dissent

DIFFERENCE — variety, diversity, medley ·

DIFFERENCE—distinction, dispute, altercation, quarrel

DIFFERENT—distinct, separate, several, divers, sundry, various, unlike

DIFFICULTIES — embarrassments, troubles, obstacles, impediments

DIFFUSE—prolix

DIGRESS—deviate

DILATE—expand

DILIGENT—expeditious, prompt

DIRECT—regulate, dispose

DIRECTION — address, superscription, order

DIRECTLY—immediately, instantly, instantaneously

DISADVANTAGE—injury, hurt, detriment, prejudice

DISAFFECTION—disloyalty

DISAPPEAR—vanish

DISAPPROVE—dislike

DISAVOW—deny, disown

DISBELIEF—unbelief

DISCERNMENT — penetration, discrimination, judgment

DISCLAIM—disown

DISCORD—strife

DISCOVER—manifest, declare

DISCREDIT — disgrace, reproach, scandal

DISCUSS—examine

DISENGAGE—disentangle, extricate

Disgust—loathing, nausea
Dishonest—knavish
Dishonor—disgrace, shame
Disjoint—dismember
Dislike—displeasure, dissatisfaction, distaste, disgust, disinclination
Dismay—daunt, appall
Dismiss—discharge, discard
Disorder—derange, disconcert, discompose, disease, distemper, malady
Disparage—detract, traduce, depreciate, degrade, decry, derogate, degrade
Disparity—inequality
Dispassionate—cool
Dispel—disperse
Dispense—distribute
Displease—offend, vex
Displeasure—anger, disapprobation
Disposal—disposition
Dispose—arrange, digest
Disposition—temper, inclination
Disregard—neglect, slight
Dissension—contention, discord
Distant—far, remote
Distinguish—discriminate
Distinguished — conspicuous, noted, eminent, illustrious
Distress—anxiety, anguish, agony, harass, perplex
Distribute—allot, assign, apportion
District—region, tract, quarter
Distrust—suspicion, diffidence
Disturb—interrupt
Divide—separate, part, distribute, share
Docile—tractable, ductile
Doctrine—precept, principle, dogma, tenet

Doubt—question, suspense
Doubtful — dubious, uncertain, precarious
Draw—drag, haul, or hale, pull. pluck, tug
Dream—reverie
Dregs—sediment, dross, scum, refuse
Dull—gloomy, sad, dismal
Durable—constant
Duration—time
Dutiful—obedient, respectful
Duty—obligation

Eager—earnest, serious
Earnest—pledge
Ease—quiet, rest, repose, easiness, facility, lightness
Easy—ready
Ebullition — effervescence, fermentation, ferment
Ecclesiastic—divine, theologian
Eclipse—obscure
Economy — frugality, parsimony, management
Economical — saving, sparing, thrifty, penurious, niggardly
Ecstacy—rapture, transport
Edifice—structure, fabric
Education—instruction, breeding
Effect—produce, perform
Effective—efficient, effectual, efficacious
Effusion—ejaculation
Elderly—aged, old
Eligible—preferable
Elocution — eloquence, oratory, rhetoric
Embarrass—perplex, entangle
Embryo—fœtus
Emissary—spy
Emit—exhale, evaporate
Empire—kingdom, reign, dominion

EMPLOY—use

EMPTY—vacant, void, devoid

ENCOMIUM—eulogy, panegyric

ENCOURAGE—animate, incite, impel, urge, stimulate, instigate

ENCOURAGE — advance, promote, prefer, forward, embolden

ENCROACH—intrench, intrude, invade, infringe

END—terminate, close, extremity

ENDEAVOR—aim, strive, struggle, effort, exertion

ENEMY—foe, adversary, opponent, antagonist

ENERGY—force, vigor

ENJOYMENT—fruition, gratification

ENLARGE—increase, extend

ENMITY—animosity, hostility

ENORMOUS—huge, immense, vast, prodigious, monstrous

ENOUGH—sufficient

ENROLL—enlist, or list, register, record

ENSLAVE—captivate

ENTERPRISING—adventurous

ENTHUSIAST—fanatic, visionary

EPITHET—adjective

EQUAL—even, equable, like, or alike, uniform

ERADICATE—extirpate, exterminate

ERROR—mistake, blunder, fault

ERUPTION—explosion

ESPECIALLY — particularly, principally, chiefly

ESSAY—treatise, tract, dissertation

ESTEEM—respect, regard

ESTIMATE—compute, rate

ETERNAL—endless, everlasting

EVADE—equivocate, prevaricate

EVASION—shift, subterfuge

EVEN—smooth, level, plain

EVENT—incident, accident, adventure, occurrence

EVIL—ill, misfortune, harm, mischief

EXACT—extort

EXACT—nice, particular, punctual

EXAMINATION—search, inquiry, research, investigation, scrutiny

EXAMINE—search, explore

EXAMPLE—pattern, ensample, precedent, instance

EXCEED—excel, surpass, transcend, outdo

EXCELLENCE—superiority

EXCESS—superfluity, redundancy

EXCESSIVE—immoderate, intemperate

EXCHANGE—barter, truck, commute

EXCITE—incite, provoke

EXCURSION—ramble, tour, trip, jaunt

EXCUSE—pardon

EXECUTE—fulfill, perform

EXERCISE—practice

EXERT—exercise

EXHORT—persuade

EXIGENCY—emergency

EXIST—live

EXIT—departure

EXONERATE—exculpate

EXPEDIENT—resource, fit

EXPERIENCE — experiment, trial, proof, test

EXPLAIN—expound, interpret, illustrate, elucidate

EXPLANATORY—explicit, express

EXPOSTULATE—remonstrate

EXPRESS—declare, signify, testify, utter

EXTEND—stretch, reach

EXTENUATE—palliate

EXTRANEOUS—extrinsic, foreign

EXTRAORDINARY—remarkable

EXTRAVAGANT — prodigal, lavish, profuse

EXTREMITY—extreme
EXUBERANT—luxuriant

FABLE—tale, novel, romance
FACE—countenance, visage
FACETIOUS—conversable, pleasant, jocular, jocose
FACTION—party
FACTIOUS—seditious
FACTOR—agent
FAIL—fall short, deficient
FAILURE — failing, miscarriage, abortion
FAINT—languid
FAIR—clear, honest, equitable, reasonable
FAITH—creed, fidelity
FAITHFUL—trusty
FAITHLESS—unfaithful, perfidious, treacherous
FALL—downfall, ruin, drop, droop, tumble
FALLACIOUS—deceitful, fraudulent
FALLACY—delusion, illusion
FAME—reputation, renown, report, rumor, hearsay
FAMILY—house, lineage, race
FAMOUS—celebrated, renowned, illustrious
FANCIFUL—fantastical, whimsical, capricious
FANCY—imagination
FARE—provision
FARMER—husbandman, agriculturist
FASTIDIOUS—squeamish
FATIGUE—weariness, lassitude
FAVORABLE—propitious
FEARFUL—dreadful, frightful,. tremendous, terrible, terrific, horrible, horrid
FEAST—banquet, carousal, entertainment, treat, festival, holiday
FEEL—sensible, conscious

FEELING—sense, sensation, sensibility, susceptibility
FEIGN—pretend
FELICITATE—congratulate
FELLOWSHIP—society
FEMALE—feminine, effeminate
FENCE—guard, security
FEROCIOUS—fierce, savage
FERTILE—fruitful, prolific
FERVOR—ardor
FESTIVITY—mirth
FICTION—fabrication, falsehood
FIGURE—metaphor, allegory, emblem, symbol, type
FINAL—conclusive
FIND—find out, discover, espy, decry, invent
FIND FAULT WITH—blame, object to
FINE—delicate, nice, mulct, penalty, forfeiture
FINICAL—spruce, foppish
FINITE—limited
FIRE—heat, warmth, glow
FIRM—fixed, solid, stable
FIT—apt, meet, equip, prepare, qualify, suit, adapt, accommodate, adjust
FIX—fasten, stick, settle, establish, determine, settle, limit
FLAG—droop, languish, pine
FLAME—blaze, flash, flare, glare
FLAT—level
FLATTERER—sycophant, parasite
FLEXIBLE—pliable, pliant, supple
FLOURISH—thrive, prosper
FLOW—stream, gush
FLUCTUATE—waver
FLUID—liquid
FOLLOW—succeed, ensue, pursue, imitate
FOLLOWER—adherent, partisan
FOLLY—foolery
FOOD—diet, regimen

Fool—idiot, buffoon

Foolhardy—adventurous, rash

Forbid—prohibit, interdict

Force—violence

Forefathers—progenitors, ancestors

Forerunners—precursors, messengers, harbingers

Foresight—forethought, forecast, premeditation

Foretell—predict, prophesy, prognosticate

Forgetfulness—oblivion

Forgive—pardon, absolve, remit

Form—figure, conformation, fashion, mould, shape, compose, constitute, ceremony, rite, observance

Formal—ceremonious, ceremonial

Formerly—in time past or old times, days of yore, anciently or ancient times

Formidable — dreadful, terrible, shocking

Forsaken—forlorn, destitute

Forswear—perjure, suborn

Fortunate—lucky, fortuitous, prosperous, successful

Foster—cherish, harbor, indulge

Found—ground, rest, build

Foundation—ground, basis

Fragile—Frail, brittle

Frame—temper, temperament, constitution

Frank—candid, ingenuous, free, open, plain

Freak—whim

Free — liberal, deliver, liberate, familiar, exempt

Freedom—liberty

Freight—cargo, lading, load, burden

Frequent—resort, haunt

Frighten—intimidate

Frolic—gambol, frank

Fulfill—accomplish, realize

Fulness—plentitude

Funeral—obsequies

Gain—profit, emolument, lucre

Gallant—beau, spark

Gape—stare, gaze

Gather—collect

Gender—sex

General—universal

Generation—age

Genteel—polite

Gentile—heathen, pagan

Gentle—tame

Get—gain, obtain, procure

Gift—present, donation, endowment, talent

Give—grant, bestow, afford, present, offer, exhibit

Give up—deliver, surrender, yield, cede, concede, abandon, resign, forego

Glad—pleased, joyful, cheerful.

Glance at—allude to

Glaring—barefaced

Gleam—glimmer, ray, beam

Glimpse—glance

Globe—ball

Gloom—heaviness

Gloomy—sullen, morose, splenetic

Glory—honor, boast, vaunt

Gloss—varnish, palliate

Godlike—divine, heavenly

Godly—righteous

Gold—golden

Good—goodness, benefit, advantage

Good-nature—good-humor

Goods—furniture, chattels, movables, effects, possession, property

Govern—rule, regulate

GOVERNMENT—administration, constitution

GRACE—favor, charm

GRACEFUL—comely, elegant

GRACIOUS—merciful, kind

GRANDEUR—magnificence

GRATIFY—indulge, humor

GRATUITOUS—voluntary

GRATUITY—recompense

GRAVE—serious, solemn, tomb, sepulchre

GREAT—large, big, grand, sublime

GRIEVANCE—hardship

GRIEVE—mourn, lament

GROAN—moan

GROSS—coarse, total

GUARANTEE—security, responsible, warrant

GUARD—defend, watch, sentinel, guardian

GUARD AGAINST—take heed

GUESS—conjecture, divine

GUEST—visitor, visitant

GUIDE—rule

GUILTLESS—innocent, harmless

GUISE—habit

GULF—abyss

HAPPEN—chance

HAPPINESS—felicity, bliss, blessedness, beatitude

HAPPY—fortunate

HARBOR—haven, port

HARBOR—shelter, lodge

HARD—firm, solid, callous, hardened, obdurate, hardy, insensible, unfeeling, difficult, arduous

HARD-HEARTED—cruel, unmerciful, merciless

HARDLY—scarcely

HASTEN—accelerate, speed, expedite, despatch, hurry

HATE—detest

HATEFUL—odious

HAUGHTINESS—disdain, arrogance

HAUGHTY—high, high-minded

HAVE—possess

HAZARD—risk, venture

HEALTHY — wholesale, salubrious, salutary

HEAP—pile, accumulate, amass

HEAR—hearken, overhear

HEARTY—warm, sincere, cordial

HEAVE—swell

HEAVY—dull, drowsy, burdensome, weighty, ponderous

HEED—care, attention

HEIGHTEN—raise, aggravate

HEINOUS—flagrant, flagitious, atrocious

HELP—assist, aid, succor, relieve

HERETIC—schismatic, sectarian, or sectary, dissenter, non-conformist

HESITATE—falter, stammer, stutter

HETERODOXY—heresy

HIDEOUS—ghastly, grim, grisly

HIGH—tall, lofty

HINDER—prevent, impede, obstruct, stop

HINT—suggest, intimate, insinuate

HIRELING—mercenary

HOLD—keep, detain, retain, occupy, possess, support, maintain

HOLINESS—sanctity

HOLLOW—empty

HOLY—pious, devout, religious, sacred, divine

HOMAGE—fealty, court

HONESTY—probity, uprightness, integrity, honor, reverence, respect, dignity

HOPE—expectation, trust, confidence

HOT—fiery, burning, ardent

HOWEVER—yet, nevertheless, notwithstanding

HUMAN—humane
HUMBLE—lowly, low, modest, submissive, humiliate, degrade
HUMOR—temper, mood, caprice
HUMORSOME—humorous, capricious
HUNT—chase
HURTFUL—pernicious, noxious, noisome
HYPOCRITE—dissembler

IDEA—thought, imagination
IDEAL—imaginary
IDLE—lazy, indolent, leisure, vacant, vain
IGNORANT — illiterate, unlearned, unlettered
ILLUMINATE—illumine, enlighten
IMITATE—copy, counterfeit
IMITATE—mimic, ape, mock
IMMINENT — impending, threatening
IMMODEST—impudent, shameless
IMPAIR—injure
IMPERFECTION—defect, fault, vice
IMPERFECTION—weakness, frailty, failing, foible
IMPERIOUS — lordly, domineering, overbearing
IMPERTINENT—rude, saucy, impudent, insolent
IMPERVIOUS—impassable, inaccessible
IMPLACABLE—unrelenting, relentless, inexorable
IMPLANT—ingraft, inculcate, instil, infuse
IMPLICATE—involve
IMPORTANCE—consequence, weight, moment
IMPRINT—impress, engrave
IMPUGN—attack
INABILITY—disability
INACTIVE—inert, lazy, slothful, sluggish

INADVERTENCE—inattention, oversight
INCAPABLE—insufficient, incompetent, inadequate
INCESSANTLY—unceasingly, uninterruptedly, without intermission
INCLINATION — tendency, propensity, proneness
INCLOSE—include
INCONSISTENT — incongrous, incoherent
INCONVENIENCE—annoy, molest
INCORPOREAL — unbodied, immaterial, spiritual
INCREASE—grow, addition, accession, augmentation
INDEBTED—obliged
INDECENT—immodest, indelicate
INDIFFERENCE—insensibility, apathy
INDIFFERENT—unconcerned, regardless
INDIGNITY—insult
INDISTINCT—confused
INDOLENT—supine, listless, careless
INDUBITABLE—unquestionable, indisputable, undeniable, incontrovertible, irrefragable
INDULGENT—fond
INFAMOUS—scandalous
INFAMY—ignominy, opprobrium
INFLUENCE—authority, ascendency, sway
INFORM—make known, acquaint, apprise, instruct, teach
INFORMANT—informer
INFORMATION—intelligence, notice, advice
INFRINGE—violate, transgress
INFRINGEMENT—infraction
INGENUITY—wit
INGENUOUS—ingenious
INHERENT—inbred, inborn, innate
INJURY—damage, hurt, harm, mischief

INJUSTICE—injury, wrong
INSIDE—interior
INSIDIOUS—treacherous
INSIGHT—inspection
INSINUATE—ingratiate
INSINUATION—reflection
INSIPID—dull, flat
INSIST—persist
INSNARE—entrap, entangle, inveigle
INSOLVENCY—failure, bankruptcy
INSPECTION—superintendency, oversight
INSTANT—moment
INSTITUTE—establish, found, erect
INSTRUMENT—tool
INSURRECTION—sedition, rebellion, revolt
INTELLECT—genius, talent
INTENT—intense
INTERCEDE—interpose, mediate, interfere, intermeddle
INTERCHANGE—exchange, reciprocity
INTERCOURSE—communication, connection, commerce
INTEREST—concern
INTERMEDIATE—intervening
INTERVAL—respite
INTERVENTION—interposition
INTOXICATION—drunkenness, infatuation
INTRINSIC—real, genuine, native
INTRODUCE—present
INTRUDE—obtrude
INTRUDER—interloper
INVALID—patient
INVASION—incursion, irruption, inroad
INVENT—feign, frame, fabricate, forge
INVEST—endure, endow
INVIDIOUS—envious

INVINCIBLE—unconquerable, insuperable, insurmountable
INWARD—internal, inner, interior
IRRATIONAL—foolish, absurd, preposterous
IRREGULAR—disorderly, inordinate, intemperate
IRRELIGIOUS—profane, impious

JANGLE—jar, wrangle
JEALOUSY—envy, suspicion
JEST—joke, make game, sport
JOURNEY—travel, voyage
JOY—gladness, mirth
JUDGE—umpire, arbiter, arbitrator
JUDGMENT—discretion, prudence
JUSTICE—equity
JUSTNESS—correctness

KEEP—preserve, save, observe, fulfil
KEEPING—custody
KILL—murder, assassinate, slay, slaughter
KINDRED — relationship, affinity, consanguinity
KNOW—be acquainted with
KNOWLEDGE—science, learning, erudition

LABOR—take pains or trouble, use endeavor
LABYRINTH—maze
LAND—country
LANGUAGE—tongue, speech, idiom, dialect
LARGE—wide, broad
LARGELY—copiously, fully
LAST—latest, final, ultimate
LASTLY—at last, at length
LAUDABLE — praiseworthy, commendable
LAUGH AT—ridicule
LAUGHABLE—ludicrous, ridiculous, comical, comic, droll

LAWFUL—legal, legitimate, licit

LAY OR TAKE HOLD OF—catch, seize, snatch, grasp, gripe

LEAD—conduct, guide

LEAN—meagre, incline, bend

LEAVE—quit, relinquish, take leave, bid farewell or adieu

LEAVE—liberty, permission, license

LEAVING—remains

LET—leave, suffer

LETTER—epistle

LETTERS—literature, learning

LIE—lay

LIFELESS—dead, inanimate

LIFT—raise, erect, elevate, exalt, heave, hoist

LIGHTNESS—levity, flightiness, volatility, giddiness

LIKENESS—resemblance, similarity, or similitude

LIKENESS—picture, image, effigy

LIMIT—extent

LINGER—tarry, loiter, lag, saunter

LIQUID—liquor, juice, humor

LIST—roll, catalogue, register

LITTLE—small, diminutive

LIVELIHOOD — living, subsistence, maintenance, support, sustenance·

LIVELY—sprightly, vivacious, sportive, merry, jocund

LIVING—benefice

LODGINGS—apartments

LOOK—glance, see, behold, view, eye, appear

LOOKER-ON — spectator, beholder, observer

LOOSE—vague, lax, dissolute, licentious

LORD'S SUPPER—eucharist, communion, sacrament

LOSE—miss

LOSS—damage, detriment

LOUD—noisy, high-sounding, clamorous

LOVE—friendship

LOVER—suitor, wooer

LOW—mean, abject

MADNESS—frenzy, rage, fury

MAGISTERIAL — majestic, stately, pompous, august, dignified

MAGNIFICENCE—splendor, pomp

MAKE—form, produce, create

MALEDICTION—curse, imprecation, execration, anathema

MALEVOLENT—malicious, malignant

MALICE — rancor, spite, grudge, pique

MANLY—manful

MANNERS—morals

MARITIME—marine, naval, nautical

MARK—print, impression, stamp, sign, note, symptom, token, indication, trace, vestige, footstep, track, badge, stigma, butt, note, notice

MARRIAGE — weddings, nuptials, matrimony, wedlock

MARTIAL—warlike, military, soldier-like

MATTER—materials, subject

MAXIM—precept, rule, law

MEAN—pitiful, sordid, medium

MEETING—interview

MELODY—harmony, accordance

MEMBER—limb

MEMORY—remembrance, recollection, reminiscence

MENTAL—intellectual, intelligent

MERCANTILE—commercial

MESSAGE—errand

MINDFUL—regardful, observant

MINISTER—agent, administer, contribute

MIRTH—merriment, joviality, jollity, hilarity

Misconstrue—misinterpret
Mix—mingle, blend, confound
Mixture—medley, miscellany
Moderation—mediocrity
Modest—bashful, diffident
Modesty—moderation, temperance, sobriety
Moisture—humidity, dampness
Money—cash
Monument — memorial, remembrancer
Motion—movement
Mournful—sad
Moving—affecting, pathetic
Multitude—crowd, throng, swarm
Mutilate—maim, mangle
Mutual—reciprocal
Mysterious—mystic

Name—call, appellation, title, denomination, style, entitle, designate, characterize, reputation, repute, credit
Natal—native, indigenous
Native—natural
Naturally—in course, consequently, of course
Necessary—expedient, essential, requisite
Necessities—necessaries
Necessity—need
Neglect—omit
Negligent — remiss, careless, thoughtless, heedless, inattentive
Negligence—(to disregard) and remissness (respect the outward action), careless, heedless, inattentive and thoughtless
Negotiate—treat for or about, transact
Neighborhood—vicinity
New—novel, modern, fresh, recent
News—tidings
Nightly—nocturnal

Noble—grand
Noise—cry, outcry, clamor
Nominate—name
Noted—notorious
Notice—remark, observe
Nourish—nurture, cherish
Numb—benumbed, torpid
Numeral—numerical

Obedient—submissive, obsequious
Object—subject, oppose
Objection—difficulty, exception
Oblong—oval
Obnoxious—offensive
Observation—observance
Observe—watch
Obstinate — contumacious, stubborn, headstrong, heady
Occasion—opportunity
Occasion—necessity
Occasional—casual
Occupancy—occupation
Odd—uneven
Offense—trespass, transgression, misdemeanor, misdeed, affront
Offender—delinquent
Offending—offensive
Offer—bid, tender, propose
Office—place, charge, function
Offspring—progeny, issue
Often—frequently
Old—ancient, antique, antiquated, old-fashioned, obsolete
Omen—prognostic, presage
One—single, only
Onward—forward, progressive
Opaque—dark
Opening—aperture, cavity
Opiniated—opiniative, conceited, egotistical
Opinion—sentiment, notion
Oppose—resist, withstand, **thwart**
Option—choice
Order—method, rule

ORIFICE—perforation

ORIGIN—original, beginning, rise, source

OUTLIVE—survive

OUTWARD—external, exterior

OVERBALANCE—outweigh, preponderate

OVERBEAR—bear down, overpower, overwhelm, subdue

OVERFLOW—inundate, deluge

OVERRULE—supersede

OVERSPREAD—overrun, ravage

OVERTURN—overthrow, subvert, invert, reverse

OVERWHELM—crush

PACE—step

PAIN—pang, agony, anguish

PAINT—depict

PALATE—taste

PALE—pallid, wan

PALPITATE—flutter, pant, gasp

PARABLE—allegory

PART—division, portion, share, piece, patch

PARTAKE—participate, share

PARTICULAR—singular, odd, eccentric, individual

PATIENCE—endurance, resignation

PATIENT—passive, submissive

PEACE—quiet, calm, tranquility

PEACEABLE—peaceful, pacific

PECULIAR—appropriate, particular

PEEL—pare

PELLUCID—transparent

PENETRATE—pierce, perforate, bore

PENETRATION—acuteness, sagacity

PEOPLE—nation, populace, mob, mobility, persons, folks

PERCEIVE—discern, distinguish

PERCEPTION—idea, conception, notion

PERISH—die, decay

PERPETRATE—commit

PERSUADE—entice, prevail upon

PICTURE—print, engraving

PILLAR—column

PITEOUS—doleful, woful, rueful

PITIABLE—piteous, pitiful

PITY—compassion, mercy

PLACE—station, situation, position, post, dispose, order, spot, site

PLAY—game, sport

PLAYFUL—gamesome, sportive

PLEASURE—joy, delight, charm

PLENTIFUL—plenteous, abundant, copious, ample

PLUNGE—dive

POISE—balance

POISON—venom

POLITE—polished, refined

POLITICAL—politic

POOR—pauper

POSITION—posture

POSITIVE—absolute, peremptory

POSSESSOR — proprietor, owner, master

POSSIBLE—practicable, practical

POVERTY—want, penury, indigence, need

POUR—spill, shed

POWER—strength, force, authority, dominion

POWERFUL—potent, mighty

PRAISE—commend, applaud, extol

PRAYER — petition, request, entreaty, suit

PRELUDE—preface

PREMISE—presume

PRESS—squeeze, pinch, gripe

PRESSING—urgent, importunate

PRESUMPTIVE—presumptuous, presuming

PRETENCE—pretension, pretext, excuse

PRETENSION—claim

PREVAILING — prevalent, ruling, overruling, predominate

PREVENT—anticipate, obviate, pre-
clude
PREVIOUS — preliminary, prepara-
tory, introductory
PRIDE—vanity, conceit, haughti-
ness, loftiness, dignity
PRIMARY—primitive, pristine, orig-
inal
PRINCE—monarch, sovereign, po-
tentate
PRINCIPLE—motive
PRIORITY — precedence, pre-emin-
ence, preference
PRIVACY—retirement, seclusion
PRIVILEGE—prerogative, exemption,
immunity
PROCEEDING — process, progress,
transaction
PROCESSION—train, retinue
PRODUCTION — produce, product,
performance, work
PROFESS—declare
PROFLIGATE—abandoned, reprobate
PROFUSION—profuseness
PROGRESS—progression, advance,
advancement, proficiency, im-
provement
PROMINENT—conspicuous
PROMISCUOUS—indiscriminate
PROMISE—engagement, word
PROOF—evidence, testimony
PROPORTIONATE — commensurate,
adequate.
PROPOSAL—proposition
PROROGUE—adjourn
PROVE — demonstrate, manifest,
evince
PROVIDE—procure, furnish, supply
PROVIDENCE—prudence
PRUDENT—prudential
PRY—scrutinize, dive into
PUBLISH—promulgate, divulge, re-
veal, disclose
PURPOSE—propose

PUSH—shove, thrust
PUT—place, lay, set

QUALIFICATION—accomplishment
QUALIFY—temper, humor
QUALITY—property, attribute
QUARREL—broil, feud, affray, fray
QUESTION—query
QUICKNESS—swiftness, fleetness,
celerity, rapidity, velocity

RACE—generation, breed
RADIANCE—brilliancy
RAPACIOUS—ravenous, voracious
RAPINE—plunder, pillage
RARE—scarce, singular
RASHNESS — temerity, hastiness,
precipitancy
RATE—proportion, ratio
RAVAGE—desolation, devastation
RAY—beam
READY—apt, prompt
REASONABLE—rational
RECEDE — retreat, retire, with-
drawn, secede
RECEIPT—reception
RECKON—count, account, number
RECLAIM—reform
RECLINE—repose
RECOGNIZE—acknowledge
RECORD—register, achieve
RECOVER—retrieve, repair, recruit
RECOVERY—restoration
RECTITUDE—uprightness
REDEEM—ransom
REDRESS—relief
REDUCE—lower
REFER—relate, respect, regard
REFORM—reformation
REFUSE—decline, reject, repel, re-
buff
RELATE—recount, describe

RELATION—recital, narration, narrative, relative, kinsman, kindred

RELAX—remit

REMAINS—relics

REMARK — observation, comment, note, annotation, commentary

REPEAT—recite, rehearse, recapitulate

REPENTANCE—penitence, contrition, compunction, remorse

REPETITION—tautology

REPREHENSION—reproof

REPRESS—restrain, suppress

REPRIEVE—respite

REPROACH—contumely, obloquy

REPROACHFULLY—abusive, scurrilous

REPROBATE—condemn

RESERVE—reservation, retain

REST—remainder, remnant, residue

RESTORATION—restitution, reparation, amends

RESTORE—return, repay

RESTRAIN—restrict

RETALIATION—reprisal

RETARD—hinder

RETORT—repartee

RETRIBUTION—requital

RETROSPECT—review, survey

RETURN—revert

REVILE—vilify

REVISAL—revision, review

REVIVE—refresh, renovate, renew

RICHES—wealth, opulence, affluence

RIDICULE—satire, irony, sarcasm

RIGHT—just, fit, proper, claim, privilege

RIPE—mature

RISE—issue, emerge

ROT—putrefy, corrupt

ROUNDNESS—rotundity

ROUTE—road, course

ROYAL—regal, kingly

RUB—chafe, fret, gall

RUPTURE—fracture, fraction

RURAL—rustic

SAFE—secure

SAGE—sagacious, sapient

SAKE—account, reason, purpose, end

SALUTE—salutation, greeting

SANGUINARY—bloody, bloodthirsty

SAP—undermine

SATISFY—please, gratify, satiate, glut, cloy

SAVE—spare, preserve, protect

SCARCITY—dearth

SCHOLAR—disciple

SCHOOL—academy

SCOFF—gibe, jeer, sneer

SCRUPLE—hesitate, waver

SEAL—stamp

SEAMAN—waterman, sailor, mariner

SECOND — support, secondary, inferior

SECRET—hidden, latent, occult, mysterious

SECULAR—temporal, worldly

SEDULOUS—diligent, assiduous

SEE—perceive, observe

SEEK—search

SEEM—appear

SELF-WILL—self-conceit, self-sufficiency

SENIOR—elder, older

SENSE—judgment

SENSIBLE—sensitive, sentient, perceptible

SENSUALIST—voluptuary, epicure

SENTENCE — proposition, period, phrase, doom, condemn

SENTENTIOUS—sentimental

SENTIMENT—sensation, perception

SEPARATE—sever, disjoin, detach

SEQUEL—close
SERIES—course
SERVANT—domestic, menial, drudge
SERVITUDE—slavery, bondage
SHADE—shadow
SHAKE—tremble, shudder, quiver, quake, agitate, toss
SHARP—acute, keen
SHINE—glitter, glare, sparkle, radiate
SHOCK—concussion
SHOOT—dart
SHORT—brief, concise, succinct, summary
SHOW—shew, point out, mark, indicate, exhibit, display, exhibition, representation, sight, spectacle, outside, appearance, semblance, parade, ostentation
SHOWY—gaudy, gay
SICK—sickly, diseased, morbid
SICKNESS—illness, indisposition
SIGN—signal, memorable
SIGNALIZE—distinguish
SIGNIFICANT—expressive
SIGNIFICATION—meaning, import, sense
SIGNIFY—imply, avail
SILENCE—taciturnity
SILENT—tacit, dumb, mute, speechless
SIMILE—similitude, comparison
SIMPLE—single, singular, simple, silly, foolish
SIMULATION—dissimulation
SINCERE—honest, true, plain
SITUATION—condition, state, predicament, plight, case
SIZE—magnitude, greatness, bulk
SKETCH—outlines
SKIN—hide, peel, rind
SLACK—loose
SLANT—slope
SLEEP—slumber, doze, drowse, nap

SLEEPY—drowsy, lethargic
SLIP—slide, glide
SLOW—dilatory, tardy, tedious
SMEAR—daub
SMELL—scent, odor, perfume, fragrance
SOAK—drench, steep
SOBER—grave
SOCIAL—sociable
SOCIETY—company
SOFT—mild, gentle, meek
SOLICITATION—importunity
SOLITARY—sole, only, single, desert, desolate
SOLVE—resolved
SOME—any
SOON—early, betimes
SORRY—grieved, hurt
SOUL—mind
SOUND—sane, healthy, tone
SPACE—room
SPEAK—say, tell, converse, discourse, talk
SPECIAL—specific, particular
SPEND—exhaust, drain, expend, waste, dissipate, squander
SPIRITUOUS — spirited, spiritual, ghostly
SPREAD—scatter, disperse, expand, diffuse, circulate, propagate, disseminate
SPRING—fountain, source, start, startle, shrink
SPRINKLE—bedew
SPROUT—bud
SPURIOUS—supposititious, counterfeit
SPURT—spout
STAFF—stay, prop, support, stick, crutch
STAGGER—reel, totter
STAIN—soil, sully, tarnish
STAND—stop, rest, stagnate
STICK—cleave, adhere

STIFLE—suppress, smother

STIR—move

STOCK—store

STORY—tale

STRAIGHT—right, direct

STRAIN—sprain, stress, force

STRAIT—narrow

STRANGER—foreigner, alien

STREAM—current tide

STRENGTHEN—fortify, invigorate

STRESS—strain, emphasis, accent

STRICT—severe

STRIFE—contention

STRIVE—contend, vie

STRONG—robust, sturdy

STUPID—dull

SUAVITY—urbanity

SUBJECT — subordinate, inferior, subservient, subjugate, subdue

SUBSIDE—abate, intermit

SUBSTANTIAL—solid

SUCCESSION—series, order

SUCCESSIVE—alternate

SUFFOCATE—stifle, smother, choke

SUPERFICIAL—shallow, flimsy

SURFACE—superfices

SURROUND — encompass, environs, encircle

SUSTAIN—support, maintain

SYMMETRY—proportion

SYMPATHY—compassion, commiseration, condolence

SYSTEM—method

TAKE—receive, accept

TALKATIVE—loquacious, garrulous

TASTE—flavor, relish, savor

TEASE—vex, taunt, tantalize, torment

TEGUMENT—covering

TEMPERAMENT—temperature

TEMPLE—church

TEMPORARY—transient, transitory, fleeting

TENACIOUS—pertinacious

THICK—dense

THIN—slender, slight, slim

THINK—reflect, ponder, muse, suppose, imagine, believe, deem

THOUGHTFUL—considerate, deliberate

THREAT—menace

TIME—season, period, age, date, era, epoch

TIMELY—seasonable

TIME-SERVING—temporizing

TORMENT—torture

TRADE—commerce, traffic, dealing

TRANSFIGURE — transform, metamorphose

TREACHEROUS—traitorous, treasonable

TREASURE—hoard

TREATMENT—usage

TREMBLING—tremor, trepidation

TRIFLING—trivial, petty, frivolous, futile

TROOP—company

TROUBLESOME—irksome, vexatious, trying

TROUBLE—disturb, molest

TRUTH—veracity

TRY—tempt

TUMULTUOUS—turbulent, seditious, mutinous, tumultuary

TURGID—tumid, bombastic

TURN—bend, twist, distort, wring, wrest, wrench, bent, wind, whirl, twirl, writhe

UNBELIEF—infidelity, incredulity

UNCOVER—discover, disclose

UNDER—below, beneath

UNDERSTANDING—intellect, intelligence

UNDETERMINED — unsettled, unsteady, wavering

UNFOLD—unravel, develop

UNHAPPY—miserable, wretched

UNIMPORTANT—insignificant, immaterial, inconsiderable

UNLESS—except

UNOFFENDING—inoffensive, harmless

UNRULY—ungovernable, refractory

UNSPEAKABLE—ineffable, unutterable, inexpressible

UNTRUTH—falsehood, falsity, lie

UNWORTHY—worthless

USAGE—custom, prescription

UTILITY—use, service, avail

UTTER — speak, articulate, pronounce

VACANCY—vacuity, inanity

VAIN—ineffectual, fruitless

VALUABLE—precious, costly

VALUE—worth, rate, price, prize, esteem

VARIATION—variety

VENAL—mercenary

VENIAL—pardonable

VERBAL—vocal, oral

VEXATION—mortification, chagrin

VIEW—survey, prospect, landscape

VIOLENT—furious, boisterous, vehement, impetuous

VISION — apparition, phantom, spectre, ghost

VOTE—suffrage

WAIT—await, look for, expect

WAKEFUL—watchful, vigilant

WANDER—to stroll, ramble, rove, roam, range

WANT—need, lack

WAVE—billow, surge, breaker

WAY — manner, method, mode, course, means

WEAK—feeble, infirm

WEAKEN—enfeeble, debilitate, enervate, invalidate

WEARISOME—tiresome, tedious

WEARY—tire, jade, harass

WEIGHT—heaviness, gravity, burden, load

WELL-BEING—welfare, prosperity, happiness

WHOLE—entire, complete, total, integral

WICKED—iniquitous, nefarious

WILL—wish

WILLINGLY—voluntarily, spontaneously

WISDOM—prudence

WIT—humor, satire, irony, burlesque

WONDER—admire, surprise, astonish, amaze, miracle, marvel, prodigy, monster

WORD—term, expression

WORK—labor, toil, drudgery, task

WRITER—penman, scribe, author

YOUTHFUL—juvenile, puerile

Taxes. An assessment; levy.

Income (Personal) tax must be paid by every citizen of the United States, whether residing at home or abroad, and by every person residing in the United States, though not a citizen thereof, having a net income of $3,000 or over for the taxable year and also by every non-resident alien deriving income from property owned and business, trade, or profession carried on in the United States by him.

Telegrams. Should be plainly written upon the form provided by the Company or attached to such form by the sender so as to leave the printed heading in full view above the telegram. Plain paper must not be used.

No charge is made for the address, hence code address is not necessary, nor accepted.

It is important to have the name of the state written in full in the address of each message directed to any city of which there are more than one of the same name.

The sender of a telegram may prepay a reply to the telegram.

A telegram containing profane, obscene or libelous language will not be accepted.

In order to facilitate the delivery of telegrams addressed to passengers en route on trains, the sender of the message should give sufficient and proper address, if possible the train number or name and the stations between which the passenger is traveling.

Messages for passengers on incoming steamers will be delivered free of charge at Quarantine if received prior to arrival of steamer.

To have a message repeated a half rate will be charged in addition to the cost of the original message.

Punctuation marks should not ordinarily be used in a telegram, and are not sent unless specific instructions are given to do so.

All numbers should be written out.

Write abbreviations F. O. B.—fob; C. O. D.—cod; etc.

Signatures are more legible when typed.

In a prepaid telegram, the following words will be counted:

All words in an extra date.

All extra words in an address (as to "John Smith, 80 Wall Street, N. Y., or James Brown, 187 Broadway, N. Y." there are eight extra chargeable words

> or
> James
> Brown
> one (1)
> eight (8)
> seven (7)
> Broadway
> Newyork.)

All words, figures and letters in the body of the telegram.

All signatures except the last one, in case of two or more.

All words after the last or only signature.

When telegrams are addressed and delivered to two or more parties they will be charged for as two or more telegrams.

"Dictionary" words (i. e., words taken from one of the following languages, namely, English, German, French, Italian, Dutch, Portuguese, Spanish and Latin), initial letters, surnames of persons, names of countries, counties, cities, towns, villages, states or territories, or names of the Canadian provinces will be counted and charged for each as one word. The abbreviations for the names of countries, counties, cities, towns, villages, states, territories and provinces will be counted and charged for the same as if written in full. Abbreviations of weights and measures in common use will be counted each as one word.

EXAMPLES.			EXAMPLES.		
Signatory (English)	1	word	New York (or N. Y.)	1	word
Auf wiedersehen (*German*)	2	"	District of Columbia (or D. C.)		
A bon marché (*French*)	3	"		1	"
Erba mala presto cresce			St. Louis		
(*Italian*)	4	"	East St. Louis		
El corazón menda las carnes			New Mexico (or N. M.)	1	"
(*Spanish*)	5	"	Nova Scotia (or N. S.)	1	"
Errare humanum est (*Latin*)			North America		
	3	"	United States	1	
J G M Jones, Jr.	5	"	United States of Colombia	1	"
Van Dorne	1	"	Queen Anne (county)	1	"
McGregor	1	"	Lbs.		
O'Connor	1	"	Hhds.		
New York State	2	"	Cwt.		

All groups of letters, when such groups do not form dictionary words and are not combinations of dictionary words, will be counted at the rate of five letters or fraction of five letters to a word. When such groups are made up of combinations of dictionary words, each dictionary word so used will be counted.

EXAMPLES.			EXAMPLES.		
Ukugu (*artificial*)	1	word	Doyou (*improperly combined*)		
Babelu (*artificial*)	2	"		2	words
Bacyzafyih (*artificial*)	2	"	Canhe (*improperly combined*)		
Abycazfybgk (*artificial*)	3	"		2	"
Hhgga (*artificial*)	1	"	Allright (or alright) (*improperly combined*)	2	"
			Housemate (*dictionary word*)	1	"

Figures, decimal points, punctuation marks and bars of division will be counted, each separately, as one word. In groups consisting of letters and figures, each letter and figure will be counted as one word.

EXAMPLES.		EXAMPLES.	
A1	2 words	4442	4 words
x9n8g	5 "	44,42	5 "
¾	3 "	1G5 East 22d St.	8 "
74¾	5 "		

EXCEPTIONS.		EXCEPTIONS.	
A. M.	1 word	C. I. F. or C. F. I	1 word
P. M.	1 "	(or cif or cfi)	1 "
F. O. B. (or fob)	1 "	C. A. F. (or caf)	1 "
C. O. D. (or cod)	1 "	O. K.	1 "
" " (quotation marks)	1 "	Per cent (or percent)	1 "
( ) (parenthesis)	1 "		

In ordinal numbers the affixes, st, nd, rd and th will each be counted as one word.

EXAMPLES.		EXAMPLES.	
1st	2 words	3rd	2 words
2nd	2 "	4th	2 "

It facilitates counting the number of words in a telegram to place five words on each line.

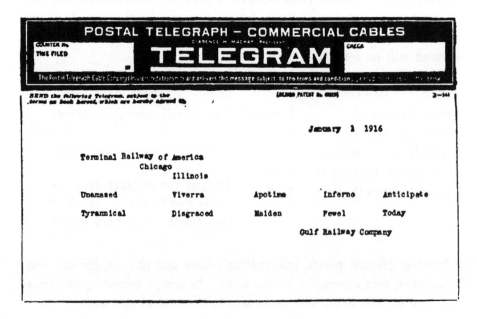

POSTAL TELEGRAPH — COMMERCIAL CABLES

CLARENCE H. MACKAY PRESIDENT

TELEGRAM

The Postal Telegraph Cable Company receives this message subject to the terms and conditions

SEND the following Telegram, subject to the terms on book hereof, which are hereby agreed to.

January 1 1916

Terminal Railway of America
Chicago
Illinois

Undamaged   Viverra   Apotime   Inferno   Anticipate

Tyramical   Disgraced   Malden   Fewel   Today

Gulf Railway Company

Translation.

Unamazed	Is my understanding correct?
Viverra	Voucher will be issued
Apotime	as soon as approved.
Inferno	Shipping instructions will be sent by mail.
Anticipate	Anticipate
Tyrannical	no trouble in regard to
Disgraced	delay caused by break in line.
Maiden	164 carloads
Fewel	went forward to destination
Today	today.

When including a quotation in a telegram, begin and end with the word "quote," as

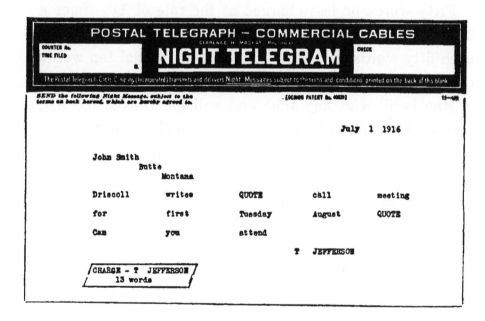

NIGHT LETTERS—The charge for Night Letters or Letter-grams of 50 words or less is the regular day rate for 10 words and 1-5 of this rate for each additional 10 words. Should be written in plain English; code or cipher not per-mitted. May be filed at any hour of the day or night up to

midnight, delivery being made as early as convenient the following morning. At option of Telegraph Company they may be mailed at destination to addressee. Artificial characters representing trade names or terms, trade designations of cotton shipments, brands or grades of flour and other manufactured products, are permissible, provided the characters are used in their natural sense and not used to convey a hidden meaning as code or cipher words do. Example: "Uneeda" (biscuit); "XXX" (brand of flour).

Day Letters—Must be written in plain English; code language not permitted.

Fifty words or less charged at the rate of 1½ times a Ten-Word Day Message Rate, and 1-5 of the initial rate for such fifty words is charged for each additional ten words or less.

May be filed at any time and will be transmitted and delivered as promptly as the Telegraph Company's facilities permit in subordination to the full paid message traffic.

Night Messages—Must be written on Night Message form.

Received after 6 o'clock p. m. for delivery the following morning, at reduced rates, but in no case less than 20 cents for a single message.

SUMMARY

of

TELEGRAPHIC RATES FROM AND TO NEW YORK CITY

(subject to change)

50-Word NIGHT LETTER RATE—same as Ten-Word DAY MESSAGE
50-Word DAY LETTER RATE—1½ times Ten-Word DAY MESSAGE

Rates for *TEN-WORD DAY MESSAGES*

Figure in parenthesis indicates rate for each word over ten.

	Cents		Cents
Alabama,	60—(4)	Nebraska,	60—(4)
Arizona,	100—(7)	Nevada,	100—(7)
Arkansas,	60—(4)	New Hampshire,	Various
California,	100—(7)	New Jersey,	25—(2)
Colorado,	75—(5)	New Mexico,	75—(5)
Connecticut,	25—(2)	New York,	Various
Delaware,	30—(2)	North Carolina,	50—(3)
Dist. of Columbia,	30—(2)	North Dakota,	75—(5)
Florida,	*60—(4)	Ohio,	40—(3)
Georgia,	60—(4)	Oklahoma,	75—(5)
Idaho,	100—(7)	Oregon,	100—(7)
Illinois,	50—(3)	Pennsylvania,	Various
Indiana,	50—(3)	Rhode Island, .	30—(2)
Iowa,	60—(4)	South Carolina,	60—(4)
Kansas,	60—(4)	South Dakota,	75—(5)
Kentucky,	†50—(3)	Tennessee,	50—(3)
Louisiana,	60—(4)	Texas,	75—(5)
Maine,	Various	Utah,	75—(5)
Maryland,	Various	Vermont,	Various
Massachusetts,	Various	Virginia,	Various
Michigan,	Various	Washington,	100—(7)
Minnesota,	60—(4)	West Virginia,	40—(3)
Mississippi,	60—(4)	Wisconsin	§60—(4)
Missouri,	‡60—(4)	Wyoming,	75—(5)
Montana,	75—(5)		

*Key West $1.00—(7).   ‡St. Louis .50—(3)
†Covington, Newport .40—(3).   §Milwaukee .50—(3)

WIRELESS—Prepaid messages are accepted for transmission at sender's risk to nearly all of the Atlantic and Pacific ocean steamships and boats, on the Great Lakes and Long Island Sound.

Notice of the sighting of an incoming steamer may be obtained from the Telegraph Company, upon application, at a cost of One Dollar in Greater New York, Hoboken and Jersey City, N. J.; all other places, an additional charge is made of tolls on one ten-word message from New York City. In New York, Brooklyn and vicinity the notice is received in time to allow friends to be at the dock when the steamer arrives. For inland places, the notice conveys the intelligence of the near approach of home-coming steamers.

Money Transferred by Telegraph. See *Money Orders.*

Telephone. An idea of the vast amount of business that is transacted over the telephone may be gained from the figures of the Bell Telephone System, which show that the number of telephone conversations held in the United States each year is greater than the combined number of telegrams and first-class letters sent through the United States mail, and that in New York City alone there are over two million telephone conversations held daily. There are in Greater New York nearly 600,000 telephones and over 7,000 telephone operators.

It is quite as important to know how to efficiently negotiate and consummate a piece of business over the telephone—voice to voice—as it is to accomplish the same at a conference—face to face.

Learn the Art of Telephony.

"The Voice With the Smile Wins" is the slogan of the New York Telephone Company.

Concentrate on what is being said over the telephone.

Speak clearly and distinctly, USING THE RISING INFLECTION.

Answer calls promptly and politely.

Courtesy of New York Telephone Company

INTERIOR OF A TELEPHONE EXCHANGE OR "CENTRAL"

Do not ask others to "Hold the Wire"; it wastes time and creates an unfavorable impression.

Use the telephone directory to make sure you have the right number; do not trust your memory.

Be slow to blame the operator for a mistake; she may not be at fault.

If you are on the wrong line, excuse yourself, remembering you have interrupted someone who is not to blame for the mistake.

The telephone reflects your personality; be yourself when telephoning.

Be courteous. Courtesy is like oil to machinery—the lack of it will cause friction. One of the surest ways of losing the regard of a person to whom you are talking, is to be inattentive to what he is saying. Concentrated, courteous attention given to a telephone conversation is a mark of respect paid to the talker that will be appreciated in most cases. Short abrupt answers or curt and impolite questions should be avoided. In practicing courtesy over the telephone, several points may be kept in mind that will be found helpful. You cannot SEE the person to whom you are talking, but the telephone reflects your accents and inflections so perfectly that you must be yourself.

In making a call, the telephone directory should be consulted in practically every case. A large percentage of the wrong connections are a direct result of a wrong number being called. For example, there are many combinations of a number with four figures—4354, 3454, 4534, etc.—

any one of these may be asked for if the memory is depended upon.

Time will be saved and annoyances avoided if the person calling identifies himself at once. "Hello", that ungraceful and rude little word that used to preface a telephone conversation, has been tabooed. The proper way to answer your telephone is to say, "Smith and Company— Miss Jones speaking." That identifies you at once and the person calling is able at once to deliver his message or ask for the particular person he wants.

If you are not the person wanted, make an effort to locate the proper person at once or politely give the information where he or she may be found. Offer to take a message and in some way show that you feel a responsibility for the proper delivery of the message.

TELEPHONE MESSAGE

Hour————————————— Date————————————

Mr.————————————— (Tel. No.————————————)

CALLED

Mr. ————————————————————————

Message—————————————————————

————————————————————————————

————————————————————————————

(Signed)————————————————————

A wide awake private branch exchange operator can do wonders to help the business of her employer. She should know how to consult the telephone directory quickly for telephone numbers that are required. She should learn to recognize the voices of customers and in answering call them by name, a courtesy that is flattering and appreciated. She should know for whom most of the incoming calls are intended and quickly switch each call to the proper person with minimum delay. New customers are always impressed with the courtesy and consideration they receive from the firm's switchboard operator.

Ticker. The machine which prints automatically, on a narrow paper tape, the prices and number of shares being sold on an exchange. These quotations are sent out from the Board Room of the Stock Exchange almost immediately after the actual transaction on the floor of the Exchange. The approval of a committee of the Stock Exchange must be obtained in order to rent one of these tickers and receive the quotations. The Produce, Cotton and other exchanges have similar machines to record their quotations and sales.

Time. See *Difference in Time.*

Ship Time—The nautical day begins at noon and is divided into "watches" of four hours each, except from 4 to 8 p. m., which time is divided into two watches of two hours each. Each hour and half hour of the day is announced by ship's bell.

The time on board ship is changed daily; in going eastward it is put forward four minutes for each degree of longitude, and in going westward it is set back four minutes for each degree.

Tonnage. Tons of freight hauled by a railroad. The freight capacity of a steamer is arrived at by finding the cubic capacity after deducting the amount of space taken up by machinery, etc.

To Wit. That is to say.

Trackage. The right of one railroad to operate its cars over the rails of another road.

Trade. Discount. A discount on the list price made to dealers.

Trademark. A special mark or emblem used by a manufacturer to represent or designate his goods, which mark, for the manufacturer's protection, is registered at the Patent Office at Washington, D. C., under the United States law relating to Trade-Marks, approved February 20, 1905 (Statutes at Large, vol. 33, part 1, pp. 724-731). A Trademark is good for thirty years.

Travelers Checks. Are a form of credit used for the convenience of travelers and the protection of their traveling funds. At the time of purchase the holder places his or her signature in the upper right hand corner of the check. This provides absolutely against loss, for the check then becomes payable only when countersigned in the lower left-hand corner by the same person in the presence of person cashing it. Comparison of the two signatures, which must agree, establishes the necessary identification. They have the advantage over a Letter of Credit, in that the Letter of Credit must be presented during banking hours, whereas a Traveler's Check is accepted generally by hotels, railroads, steamship lines, merchants, shop-keepers, etc., at its face value in gold or its equivalent in the money of the country where accepted, and may be cashed on Sundays, holidays or fête-days either before or after business hours.

These checks are a convenience abroad or for tourists in Canada and the United States.

A REDUCED FACSIMILE OF A $10 TRAVELER'S CHECK.

Trust Company. Any domestic corporation formed for the purpose of taking, accepting and executing such trusts as may be lawfully committed to it, and acting as trustee in the cases prescribed by law, and receiving deposits of moneys and other personal property, and issuing its obligations therefor, and of loaning money on real or personal securities.

Trust Deed. See *Deeds.*

Type.

6 pt. Caslon Oldstyle.   An interesting feature of the work is that it keeps us the greater par

6 pt. Bookman Oldstyle.   This is the place that I cherished since the day

8 pt. Ronaldson Oldstyle.   If we please you tell your friends

8 pt. Cheltenham Oldstyle.   If we please you tell your friends, if not, tell us

10 pt. Cheltenham Bold.   This type is popular

10 pt. Caslon Bold.   At the time the outcome

12 PT. PLATE GOTHIC.   THESE

12 PT. ENGRAVERS RO

14 pt. Litho Roman.   Between

14 PT. ENGRAVER

18 pt. Tudor Black.   Twenty

18 pt. Engravers Old English.   It

Underwrite.   To subscribe to, or undersign.

To UNDERWRITE insurance is to issue policies of insurance. See *Lloyds*. To UNDERWRITE an issue of stocks or bonds is to subscribe to all or part of the same. See *Syndicate*.

Usury.   An interest charge exceeding the legal rate. See *Interest*.

Valid.   Legal; legitimate; lawful.

Venue.   Neighborhood. "Change of venue"—change of district in which a case is to be tried.

Verification. An affirmation sworn to by a party to an action that what he has stated is true to the best of his knowledge and belief.

FORM OF VERIFICATION.

CITY OF...................... }
  ss:
COUNTY OF.................... }

....*being duly sworn,*
says that he is the...*herein,*
that the foregoing ....*is true to his own*
knowledge, except as to the matters which are therein stated to be
alleged on information and belief, and as to those matters be believes it
to be true.

Sworn to before me, this............... }
    day of....................191 }

Verbatim. Word for word.

Void. Illegal, not binding, without effect, not good.

Voucher. Receipt.

Voucher Check. See *Checks.*

Waiver. The giving up of a right.

Wall Street. A street in the downtown section of New York City, running from Broadway to the East River, on which is located the United States Sub-Treasury, many large banking houses and in close proximity to which is the Stock Exchange. It is the financial center of the United States, and in this connection WALL STREET is often referred to as meaning the national money market or financial interests of the country as a whole. Threadneedle, Throgmorton and Lombard Streets in England have a similar significance.

In the early days, when New York (Manhattan) belonged to the Dutch, Wall Street was the site of a fortified wall which formed the southern defence to the city, from which it is named.

At its head, on Broadway, old Trinity Church, where George Washington is said to have worshipped, still stands, and a statue of Washington in front of the Sub-Treasury marks the spot on which he delivered his first inaugural address.

Warrant.   An order.   A writ of arrest or search.

Warranty Deed.   See *Deeds.*

Watered Stock.   See *Bonds and Stocks.*

Weights and Measures.

AVOIRDUPOIS WEIGHT.

27½	Grains	= 1 Drachm (dr.) or	27½	Grains
16	Drachms	= 1 Ounce (oz.) or	437½	"
16	Ounces	= 1 Pound (lb.) or	7000	"
25	Pounds	= 1 Quarter (qr.).		
4	Quarters	= 1 Hundredweight (cwt.)		
20	Cwts.	= 1 Ton.		
2000	Pounds	= 1 Short Ton.		
2240	Pounds	= 1 Long Ton.		

Apothecaries' Weight.

20 Grains = 1 Scruple.   8 Drachms = 1 Ounce.
3 Scruples = 1 Drachm.   12 Ounces = 1 Pound.

Diamond Weight.

16 Parts = 1 Grain (4-5ths Grain Troy.)
4 Grains = 1 Carat (3 1-5th Grains Troy.)

Troy Weight.

24 Grains   = 1 Pennyweight, or   24 Grains.
20 Pennywts.   = 1 Ounce,   or   480   "
12 Ounces   = 1 Pound,   or 5760   "

Minimum Weights of Produce.

The following are minimum weights of certain articles of produce according to the laws of the United States:

Per Bushel.		Per Bushel.	
Wheat	60 lbs.	Dried Peaches	33 "
Corn, in the ear	70 "	Dried Apples	26 "
Corn, shelled	56 "	Clover Seed	60 "
Rye	56 "	Flax Seed	56 "
Buckwheat	48 "	Millet Seed	50 "
Barley	48 "	Hungarian Grass Seed	50 "
Oats	32 "	Timothy Seed	45 "
Peas	60 "	Blue Grass Seed	44 "
White Beans	60 "	Hemp Seed	44 "
Castor Beans	46 "	Salt (see note below).	
White Potatoes	60 "	Corn Meal	48 "
Sweet Potatoes	55 "	Ground Peas	24 "
Onions	57 "	Malt	34 "
Turnips	55 "	Bran	20 "

Salt.—Weight per bushel as adopted by different States ranges from 50 to 80 pounds. Coarse salt in Pennsylvania is reckoned at 80 pounds, and in Illinois at 50 pounds per bushel. Fine salt in Pennsylvania is reckoned at 62 pounds, in Kentucky and Illinois at 55 pounds per bushel. —*World Almanac.*

Cubic Measure.

1728 Cubic Inches = 1 Cubic Foot.
27 Cubic Feet   = 1 Cubic Yard.

CIRCULAR MEASURE.

60	Seconds	=	1 Minute
60	Minutes	=	1 Degree
30	Degrees	=	1 Sign
90	Degrees	=	1 Quadrant
4	Quadrants	=	12 Signs
360	Degrees	=	1 Circle

CLOTH MEASURE.

2¼	Inches	=	1 Nail
4	Nails	=	1 Quarter
4	Quarters	=	1 Yard

DRY MEASURE.

2 Pints = 1 Quart		8 Bushels = 1 Quarter.
8 Quarts = 1 Peck.		36 Bushels = 1 Chaldron.
4 Pecks = 1 Bushel.		1 Bushel = 2150.42 Cubic Inches.

LINEAR MEASURE.

12	Inches	=	1 Foot
3	Feet	=	1 Yard
5½	Yards	=	1 Rod
40	Rods	=	1 Furlong
8	Furlongs	=	1 Mile
5280	Feet	=	1 Mile
3	Miles	=	1 League

LIQUID MEASURE.

4 Gills = 1 Pint.		31½ Gallons = 1 Barrel.
2 Pints = 1 Quart.		63 Gallons = 1 Hhd.
4 Quarts = 1 Gallon.		252 Gallons = 1 Tun.

MARINER'S MEASURE.

6	Feet	=	1 Fathom
120	Fathoms	=	1 Cable Length
7½	Cable Lengths	=	1 Mile
5280	Feet	=	1 Statute Mile
6085	Feet	=	1 Nautical Mile

Paper Measure.

24 Sheets	=	1 Quire
20 Quires	=	1 Ream
2 Reams	=	1 Bundle
5 Bundles	=	1 Bale

Square Measure.

144	Square Inches	=	1 Square Foot.
9	Square Feet	=	1 Square Yard.
30¼	Square Yards	=	1 Square Rod, Perch or Pole.
40	Square Rods	=	1 Rood.
4	Roods	=	1 Acre.
	Gunter's Chain	=	22 Yards or 100 Links.
10	Square Chains	=	1 Acre.
640	Acres	=	1 Square Mile.
272¼	Square Feet	=	1 Square Rod.
43,560	Square Feet	=	1 Acre.

Surveyors' Measure.

7.92	Inches	=	1 Link
25	Links	=	1 Rod
4	Rods	=	1 Chain
10	Square Chains		
	or		
160	Square Rods	=	1 Acre
640	Acres	=	1 Square Mile
36	Square Miles	=	1 Township

Time Measure.

60 Seconds	=	1 Minute
60 Minutes	=	1 Hour
24 Hours	=	1 Day
7 Days	=	1 Week
28, 29, 30 or		
31 Days	=	1 Calendar Month
30 Days	=	1 Interest Month
365 Days	=	1 Year
366 Days	=	1 Leap Year

Wills. All persons who have attained the age of eighteen years and are of sound mind and memory may make a will.

In most states the will must be in writing, signed by the testator with two attesting witnesses who must sign in the presence of the testator and of each other.

The wording or form is immaterial, so long as the intention of the testator is clear.

A second will invalidates a former one, provided it contains words expressly revoking it.

A bequest is often made by a man to his wife in "lieu of dower," the one-third she is entitled to receive by law. See *Release of Dower*.

EXECUTOR—(or executrix—fem.). One who is nominated in the will to carry out its provisions.

ADMINISTRATOR—(or administratrix—fem.). One who is appointed to distribute the property of an intestate. The next of kin is usually given preference.

SHORT FORM OF WILL.

I............................., of ....
.... County ....being of *sound and disposing mind and memory, but mindful of the uncertainties of this life, do hereby make, publish and declare this to be my Last Will and Testament, in manner and form following, that is to say:*
FIRST: I direct that all my just debts, funeral and testamentary expenses be paid as soon after my decease as conveniently can be done.
SECOND: I give and bequeath to

etc., etc.

*I hereby nominate, constitute and appoint.........................
sole executor of this my Will and I hereby revoke all former and other wills by me made and declare this and this only to be my last Will and Testament.*

In Witness Whereof *I have hereunto set my hand and seal this*
.... *day of* .... *nineteen hun-*
dred ....

....(*L.S.*)

Subscribed, sealed, published and declared
by .... *as and for her last*
Will and Testament, in the presence of each
of us, who, at her request, in her presence,
and in the presence of each other have here-
unto subscribed our names as witnesses this
.... *day of* .... *19....*

.... *residing at* ....
.... *residing at* ....

CODICIL—Is an addition or alteration to a will.

This is a codicil to my last will and testament dated..........

Whereas *by my said will, I have given*...........................
all my ....*I now declare that it is my*
will that instead of that provision she shall have......................
And I hereby revoke the appointment of ....
.... *to be one of my executors, and I*
appoint.....................................*to take that office, with*
all the powers and duties in my said will declared.

In Witness Whereof *I have hereunto set my hand this*.........
.... *day of* ....*19....*

(*Signature*)

(*Attestation clause*
Signature of witnesses.)

PROBATE—As soon as possible after the death of the testator the will should be probated (proved); that is, the witnesses, if living, should appear before the proper court
and testify as to its genuineness.

Without   See *Notes.*
Recourse.

This book is DUE on the last date stamped below

Lightning Source UK Ltd.
Milton Keynes UK
UKHW020958200219
337611UK00014B/924/P